Dedicated to my daughter, Theresa Walker (nee Bird)
who died of cancer aged 47.
Dearly loved and missed.

A Walk Down Memory Lane

- A memoir by Frank Bird -

35. A Walk Down Memory Lane

1. My First Recollection

The first recollection which sticks out in my mind was when I was four years old. We had just moved from Barnsley Road where I was born to live in a newly built house. Our new address was 21 Jardine Street in Wombwell, located near Barnsley. My parents were called Alathea and Thomas Bird. They had six children, three boys and three girls. In order of age there was Harold, Hilda, Leslie, Gwendoline, Lillian and myself, the youngest, Frank. Our new home was in a row of four council houses which were split in the centre by an entry which was also known as a ginnel. We children called it 'a good place to hide' whether we were in trouble or just playing games. It was a place that might teach you why the girls wore frocks and why the boys wore short trousers during games of hide and seek.

It was Bonfire Night and at the back of our house in the next street, the Ives family were setting off fireworks. The Ives were comprised of Mr Ives, who was a widower, and his children Beatrice, Edward, Hilda and Henry. The latter had been unfortunately born with a hunchback. The Roman Candles lit up our back garden, beckoning me to come closer, so I did. Unfortunately on my treck down the garden I fell over my mother's old tin trunk which she had used to 'sally forth into the great unknown' when she first went into service. She had brought it up from the old Barnsley Road house when we flitted and promptly planted it with dandelions, declaring that it 'deserved a bouquet'.

The rest of the firework show I viewed from the top of the kitchen table which our Leslie pushed up to the window. Standing there, holding a flannel to each bleeding knee I thought, 'Living in this life is going to hurt if you're not careful!'

2. The Music Box

Our branch of the Bird family originated in Oldbury, a town in Staffordshire, where they took part in the wire industry as Wire-Drawers. Some of the family however worked in the coalmines in that region. My father told me that William Bird, his father, could neither read nor write, but he could see and hear. He had heard about Yorkshire Miners starting a Trade Union in Barnsley. These were a band of men who asked for, and sometimes got, justice from the coal owners. So he thought he'd try to get his workmates interested in doing the same for their industry. Unfortunately word got to the wire industry owners, who promptly sacked him. They also blackballed him, making sure he couldn't get a job anywhere else in that area.

So he decided to go to Yorkshire, where men were at least listened to. Having no money, he walked all the way from the West Midlands, lying under hedge bottoms, in haystacks and in fields at night to sleep. Dad told me that Will had often gone hungry on his walk but that he found some odd jobs along the way when he could, which enabled him to eat something. He was born in 1850 at Round Green in Worcestershire and married Sarah Malin, a butcher's daughter who was born in 1851 at Hilltop in Staffordshire. She went to live with her father while her husband went to find a job in Yorkshire until William eventually ended up at Grimethorpe. He had heard that men were wanted there and, when set on and established, he found a home for them both at 29 Jones Cottage, Scar Field, Ardsley.

So started the Bird dynasty in Yorkshire. They settled down and produced five daughters, namely Martha, Maria, Lily, Elsie and Emma. They also had three sons and named them Joseph, Richard and Thomas, or Tommy as he was more often called, who was my father. The men of the family worked as Colliers at the Grimethorpe Collier on a heading which was eventually called 'Bird's Level'. They were happy all working together for several years, until someone decided that Tommy Bird was somebody special and offered him the job as the 'Traffic Manager'. He wanted to stay where he was and refused to move, and so he was told to go find a job elsewhere.

After that Tommy found work at Cortonwood Colliery and moved his wife, whom by this time he had met and married, and my brothers and sisters into a terraced house at Wombwell, on Barnsley Road. In time all his brothers joinned him and together they helped him get a position on the Yorkshire Miners' Union Board. At first he was just on the Committee, but then was made Treasurer and after that the Secretary. The Union meetings were held at a public house called The Guide Post once a fortnight.

When he was the Treasurer, his Secretary was none other than Joseph Arthur Hall, who went on to become the President of the Yorkshire Miners' Union. Joseph Arthur became famous for his actions when an impasse was met with the Coal Owners. He went up to the Winding Houses and told the 'Winders' to make their engines safe and to get off their winding stools. That stopped all production for the entire pit and it was surprising how quickly the problem got sorted out after that.

Tommy went on to inaugurate the 'Cortonwood Miners' Home Coal Scheme'. This was where coal was delivered to the Miners' homes as part of their wages. Despite this the Colliers didn't seem to have a lot of time for his preaching, but he had a lot of time for his Union members. Later on when he put his name forward to be a Labour Councillor he was duly elected for the North Ward of Wombwell Council. As a result I didn't see a lot of him as a child, as during his time working for the Council he had to go to lots of conferences in different parts of the country. When he did he would always try to bring me a toy back though.

I remember one of the presents was a working model of the seaplane which had won the Shnieder Trophy that year, but it didn't have a long trip in our bath before its propellers stopped turning around. The one present however that will always stay in my mind was a toy gramophone. It wasn't very big but to my mind it was marvellous. Contained in a bright blue box, which had on each side a different type of instrument depicted, was a small turntable, a sound box which also held the needle and a lever for regulating the speed. Every working part could be lowered into the box when the lid had to be closed. It was a work of art just to see for me and the music it played that fascinated me.

There was just one record, but for a little boy my age it didn't need anymore. One side played 'In A Persian Market' and the other one, 'In A Monastery Garden' which were both written by Albert William Ketelbey. To my mind he was a composer who has never been bettered in writing picture music - that's what Billy and I used to say anyway.

I used to sit on the back door step with rapture thinking, 'Which picture shall I see first today?' and then I would open the lid. The winding handle was clipped to the inside of the lid and the record was on the turntable. So, when you had put the handle into the winding hole and wound it ten times, (no more or no less according to the instructions,) you were ready. I was just at this point in the proceedings one day when I heard a little cough. When I looked up, there at my side, was my mirror image. The only difference was that his little woollen tie had a red stripe to my own blue one. He had brown curly hair, brown eyes and a worried look on his bonny little face. "Is it all right if I come to play?" he asked timidly. "I've seen you over your wall and always wanted to". And that was the start of a great friendship.

I showed him how the gramophone worked and he told me that his name was Billy Bradley and that he lived at the top of Mellor Road. We took it in turn to do every operation of the gramaphone and choose in turn which tune was to be played. Then we told each other what we'd pictured whilst listening to it. He told me that he had no brothers or sisters, just his Mum and Dad, and asked if he could always come to play.

So we sat day in, day out, on either side of the step with the music box in the middle, talking of the sights we would imagine after each piece of music. The stately line of camels coming in from the desert, drivers by their sides and their harness bells tinkling, each with a different sound. Each loaded with goods to sell in the market; carpets, sheepskins, ornaments and foodstuffs of every description. Then we were in the market, inhalling the smells and hearing the sounds. Newly baked bread, food being prepared and the smell of a thousand people packed together. There were beggars shouting 'Alms for the love of God!', jostled out of the way for their trouble, silversmiths cross-legged tapping away designing trays and cups, and the cries of stallholders asking people to look at or sample their wares. But what we both marvelled at were the colours, every one brilliant and of every hue imaginable. And how did people make them?!

Then, when we had finished discussing the excitement of the market, it was the turn of the solitude and quietness of a monastery, surrounded by green lawns, trees and all the beautiful gardens. In the distance we heard the voices of the monks singing. The world was at peace and so were we. Billy came up to play at least twice a week without fail, so when he didn't come around it made me think he must be ill, or even worse, I wondered if his family had moved.

The next morning I was sitting on the back door step with my music box awaiting Billy when my Dad came outside. I asked him where he thought Billy could be. He looked down at me sadly and said, "Billy's dead and gone to glory". The cold step had never affected me before, but at these words I froze to the bone. "But why him Dad? Billy never harmed anyone, why Billy?" Dad just shook his head, turned round and walked off. I knew what I had to do then. After packing the gramophone up, each part in its place, I got some brown paper and string and made it into a parcel. The only place where nobody would look for it I thought, would be the 'Cistern Room' which was a cupboard housing the hot water tank in the back bedroom. And so that's where I hid it. Billy and I had spent so many happy hours together listening to our music box that I simply couldn't bring myself to play it without him.

3. The Early Days

As a child my two brothers, Harold and Leslie, slept on either side of me in our bed. This was for a time in the back bedroom which housed the Cistern Room. When hot water was used in the kitchen, cold water replaced it, making a gurgling noise in the cistern. That was, my two loving brothers told me, 'The Cistern Man' and it filled me with dread whenever I heard it as they told me that if I didn't keep still and quiet he would come out of his room and get me! I was all right when they were in the bed with me, but when I was on my own I was more than a little worried! I never saw the parcel in its corner behind the Cistern Room door again however, even when I grew old enough to work out that there wasn't a bogey man in there waiting to get me.

My mother, Alathea, suffered with a heart trouble so as Hilda was the eldest she had to be a second mother to us. It was the usual practice in those days. The elder daughter was expected to look after the younger children. She was a very clever girl and if you wanted help in any shape or form she was always ready and willing to aid you. When the time for me to start school came, Hilda was the one who showed me how to tie my shoelaces, making sure that I pulled them tight so that they didn't unfasten.

My father took me to the King's Road School on my first day as a scholar and all the teachers seemed to know him. I really didn't mind being left by him as the big room was filled with little boys and girls, every one of them doing interesting things. There were big boxes of sand and children making roads and castles out of it, and teachers telling them to 'Keep it in the box!' The smell of plasticine filled the air as the budding sculptors pounded it into a pulp. Everybody who either played with water or painted got a little pinafore to wear so I asked for one. And that's how I was introduced to school and later that same morning inagurated into the daily ritual of school milk with two ginger biscuits which seemed an unimaginable treat.

One hardship about being at school, and a lesson I quickly learnt, was never to drink out of our cold water taps at playtime. Some children didn't get milk at break time. Instead they were given a dreaded dose of cod liver oil by the School Nurse. The first thing they did of course, was run to the sinks in the toilets where they got rid of it and had a drink to get the taste out of their mouths. That meant that if you wanted a drink then you were forced to wait until you got home.

There were two boys who I was friendly with at school, namely Jimmy Sadler and Frank Steele. They both lived on the opposite side of the road to us. We used to dig all over Steele's garden in our never-ending search for coal and, as it kept us quiet, we were allowed to! I suppose that our notion was that we would be coal miners when we left school, so we might as well get some practice in while we had some spare time. Both boys were the only children their parents had and thought I was so lucky having brothers and sisters. They should have tried sleeping with Les and Harold and the rumble of the Cistern Man!

Our Harold was known to tell a few untruths occasionally just to be the centre of attraction, so Leslie called him 'Lothario'. Once I asked Les why he called him that and he told me that Lothario was an Italian man who couldn't stop chasing women and he told lies a lot. Come to think of it looking back, that was our 'Loathie', (for that's what we called him,) to a tee. He'd have the girl next door shining his shoes just so he could go out and meet another one on the town. I often wondered where our Les got all his information from because he was always right, and why did all the girls believe what Loathie said? It could have been of course because he was a 'Dapper Dan' and always dressed smartly. Never at a loss for something to say, and it was usually amusing when he said it.

My nickname, according to Les, was Frankie Darro. He got it from 'The Penny Rushes' which we went to when he came home from school at the Hippodrome. You could either pay a penny to get in or two jam jars. The reasoning behing it I'm sure that the people who owned the Jam Factory in Wombwell had some shares in the 'Hip', as we called it. Les used to carry me there on his back, me eating a slice of bread and jam with one hand and holding on to his neck with the other. There were just plain wooden tip-up seats at the front where we sat which weren't very comfortable until you got carried away with the film and then you didn't feel a thing. There were two more cinemas in Wombwell - the Pavilion down Marsh Street and the Empire at the bottom of the Feast Field. But the one that was dearest to our hearts, and the nearest, was the Hip.

Our Leslie was good at giving people nicknames. He called our Gwen, who had a snub nose 'Puggy'. Lillian, who from early childhood had a tendency to tell on people, he christened 'Isher Doo', as she used to say "Isherdoo I shall tell," and she always did. Les never dared give Hilda a nickname though.

When I got a little older the girls took me on walks and showed me where the 'Hilly Fields' were, which became my happy hunting grounds. We also went to the nearest seaside resort to us, *Elsecar by the Sea*. It was quite a walk so I was often pushed in my old pram. Our provisions were sandwiches and bottles of water. The journey took us straight up to the Park Top and then down the fields past the Three Oaks.

When we had passed the resevoir on the left hand side into which the famrer's fields drained, or 'Rezzer' as we called it, we went straight up the fields to Hemingfield, which was a very steep climb. Then we turned right and walked down to Tingle Bridge Lane where it was all down hill to the railway crossing at the bottom. All the coal mined at Elsecar Main was transported on these rails which ended up at the Wath Hump to be sent to its destination, which could be anywhere in the world. The crossing had two hinged gates which guarded whichever side that was wanted to be used and a Mr and Mrs Moulds were in charge of it.

We then turned right to walk up yet another hill and passed the Pumping Pit which 'Lordie' or the Earl Fitzwilliam had caused to be sunk. The shaft had pumps at its bottom which kept the mine water out of both of his Elsecar Main Colliery and the New Stubbin Colliery. Miners at these collieries praised him for his generosity as he gave them a dinner at Wentworth House once a year in the Servant's Quarters on wooden plates, but that was only if they'd brought their own knives and forks. There were grumblings however as there was never a pudding, but it was a reward of sorts for bringing a whole year's rent to him.

Our journey then took us past Elsecar Main on our left, over the canal bridge on our right and then left towards the Flour Mill. After that it was straight forward, passing Lordie's Workshops on the way, and we were at the Elsecar Park gates. We then had to walk through the Park to get to the paddling pool which was at the end of Elsecar Reservoir.

On the occasion I can recall the weather was fine and warm when we got there. Children were ringing the pool and quite a few were paddling. There were four steps into the pool, three of which had a drop of six inches but the last one was only three. Of course if you hadn't used it before then it often meant an early 'Bath Night', fully dressed and very cold too! The children at the poolside were counting the bathers who had fallen in. I was number twenty-one. We didn't stay very long after that. Our Gwen pulled me out and I had to walk home all the way to make sure I was dry when we arrived.

To make sure that I was definitely dry on this occasion I was forced to walk up through Hemingfield which was the long way round to the Hilly Fields. In doing so we passed on our right Lundhill Row, houses used for the workmen at Lundhill Colliery before an explosion caused it to close. One hundred and eighty night men and boys had lost their lives due to Firedamp exploding one cold February day in 1857. As we passed by the site we saw the granite slabs which were still lying where the force of the blast had thrown them. They had been part of the Head Gear and when you saw the size of them, the sheer force of the blast which had thrown them so far was clear. Hilda pointed out the communal grave where all the victims had been buried and later on to my disgust, I found out that coach loads of tourists would actually come to visit the site where it had happened.

Gradually as I grew older my wanderings took me down the Hilly Fields with boys who lived near me. We couldn't get away from school quick enough, running home to have a 'biting on' or a bit of food, and then away to adventure. Our playground belonged to Wombwell Urban District Council and they didn't seem to have found a use for it at that time of the day, but we did. If you were really feeling fit we could walk down to the reservoir at the fields.

On these occasions if we were really quiet when we got to the water then sometimes we would see a newt on the surface. Then, if you were quick enough, you could slip your hand underneath it and flip it onto the bank. A jam jar was a must when going on one of these trips - just in case you were lucky enough to catch something. I remember catching a newt once and proudly taking it home. It was fully grown and had bright pink eyes. It could also turn and climb up its own tail. I made the mistake of showing him off whilst my youngest sister Lillian was in the room and of course she screamed her head off and she told on me yet again. The inevitable happened, as Mum degreed it was to be returned straight away to where it came from. As I didn't fancy the long trek back, I put it down our grate in the yard. When I came back too quickly for Lillian, she demanded to know where I'd put it. When she found out she wished she had never asked. For a long time after that she slept downstairs swearing that she knew horrible things like that could climb drainpipes.

We, that is to say my friends and I, played cricket and football on the Well Pitch which was against Lodge's House. This was built in the middle of the Hillies at the bottom of a steep clay cliff. In the centre of the pitch was a square brick building which housed the well which the pitch took its name from. There the Lodge family would collect their water through a door in the side, lowering a bucket on a rope. During the summer months they sold sweets and lemonade from a wooden guard van outside their house. I spent a lot of time there, lying in the grass and watching birds during the summer. I would find where their nests were and filled quite a few tin boxes of eggs, laying them on cotton wool. There was also a pond halfway up the Hillies which always had frogs in. We used to catch them, make a racetrack and pit them against each other. They were happy days and seemed to last forever, and it was only time to wend our way home when it started to get dark.

4. The Next Chapter

School had altered after that first summer. We had long since stopped playing and instead had started learning and I didn't like it as much as I used to. It could have been partly because we had a new boy start at the school. I'll call him B.F. and he had a harelip. The first time I saw him pity must have shown on my face. It was the worst thing I could have done and so I suffered for it the next day. When I got to school in the morning he was waiting behind the gate with a belt in his hand. It was striped in red, black and white with a metal snake clip at the end. When I walked through the gate into the playground he showed me why he was waiting, with a smart crack to my bottom with the belt. I couldn't believe it but didn't wait for explanations and shot off.

That's why I used to drag my feet down Mellor Road to school and pray for the weekend to come round. The teachers must have seen what was happening but turned a blind eye. They probably thought that in time I would be trained up to outpace him. Lillian, my sister, threatened to tell my mother about it, but changed her mind when I mentioned newts. After a week or two however, with B.F. being a podgy sort of a lad, I could outpace him easily and just let him have a strike when he was exhausted. Suddenly then one morning he wasn't at school anymore. I never found out where he went but I was certainly sorry for the children at his next school!

Lillian and I went to a Sunday school at the Primitive Methodist church in Park Street. But we didn't stay long as it had a Superintendent who we called Knuckles for obvious reasons. If you didn't keep your 'stars' coming in on your 'Star Card' regularly he stamped your skull with his knuckles. Lillian had some friends at school who got her to go with them to the Church of England and so I was asked to go as well. If you were a boy and belonged to the 'Church without a Steeple', (which wasn't very far from our house,) you could join the Church Lads Brigade.

Being in the Lads Brigade was nothing like school. We formed into four lines and marched behind a band. It was composed of four kettledrums and six trumpets and you felt very proud to be in it. That was until one night in the Church Hall when we played a new game, one which would give us 'Backbone'. That's what the Officer said. About twenty of us boys were told to form a ring, facing towards the centre and to bend over. Then I heard a noise that filled me full of dread, a crack of a belt on somebody's bottom. 'I've done this before and I'm not going to do it again,' I thought. Two boys ran around the outside of the circle, one chasing the other one with a belt in his hand. He cracked his victim whenever he could until they got back to their respective places. Then the victim got the belt and walloped the boy next to him. So it continued, until it came to my turn to get whopped. I broke all the rules.

Snatching the belt from my assailant I threw it into the centre of the ring. The boy at the side of me must have thought it was Christmas because I gave him a slight tap on his bottom. Then I chased him round the ring until the door was opposite, then it was freedom! No more would I march to the rattle of the kettledrums and the blare of the copper plated bugles because I never went back, but I did think B.F.'s Dad must have been in the Lads Brigade at some point.

5. Just Frank

There was a sequel to this story, when I saw B.F. for the last time. I was married and living in Hemingfield. On walking past the Elephant and Castle I saw B.F., now sporting a large moustache, with a young couple outside the pub. 'Now then,' I thought, 'I'll get even for all the beltings he gave me!' because he was standing at the side of the Canal. He only needed a push and would have an early bath, to ease some of my early discomforts. I started to go towards him but then thought about the result of my actions. 'It isn't worth it,' I decided. 'I'd have to get him out anyways afterwards and would probably end up in court for my trouble.' So I walked away with a light heart thinking I wouldn't have to go to court ever.

To get back to my school days, my best subject was English and I used to love to read. Friday couldn't come around quickly enough for me as that afternoon we had 'Book Club'. All the pupils in the class had to pay half a crown and then could choose a book that they would like to read. I always chose 'Just William' books and devoured them. We had all Friday afternoon set apart to read our books and exchange them. The author of the 'Just William' books was someone called Richmal Crompton which sounded a very masculine name to me. I was exteremely surprised to find out later on that the author was in fact a woman. I couldn't believe it! How on earth could she ever have known what went on in a boy's mind? I found out later that the woman had once been a girl who had had lots of brothers; she must have watched them very closely indeed.

In due time I worked my way out of the Infants and went up into the Juniors and met new children. One of these was called Peggy, a little girl who I thought was very pretty. She lived on Jardine Street, about five houses on from ours, on the other side of the road. We seemed to like each other at first sight, walking around the playground telling each other about ourselves. Her Dad worked on the railway, a signalman who worked in a signal box. But, unfortunately, they didn't stay long in the area. I never forgot her however.

When you moved up into the Juniors class and it was around August time, in the afternoon a terrific noise would nearly deafen you. But it didn't alarm anybody. All the rattling, grinding and chuffing told you that it had arrived at last! Harry Tuby's Traction Engines were on the road outside the school, pulling all the fun of the fair behind them. Wombwell Feast had arrived and the Feast Ground was opposite the school. I would run home from school on that day, have my tea and get back quickly to watch intently how it was put together. I wasn't really bothered about going on the roundabouts but would stand forever by the traction engine, marvelling how a belt, from its flywheel turned a dynamo generating electricity. This was of course the fair's life-blood. Cables ran all over the ground to the different amusements so you had to watch where you walked. When everything was built up at night a rosy glow filled the sky. Then you knew it was time to walk down to the Feast Field, which didn't take long, as it was at the bottom of our street.

When you walked through the gate on the left hand-side you came across the first ride, or should I say *The Frightener*. It was also called Pullen's Steam Boats. Two huge brightly painted boats hung on a massive frame. Mr or Mrs Pullen would fire up a boiler which was positioned between them providing steam, which in turn operated two pistons, causing the boats to swing to terrifying angles. If you were very brave, (or a little bit tipsy,) you climbed up the wooden steps which were on both sides to get into either boat.

There was a rope netting which was draped inside which protected you if the swing swung when your hands weren't holding on to the plank seat. Each boat carried about sixty people, so you can imagine the groans and screams when they went to the top. The boat trip was accompanied by a steam organ which played appropriate tunes; 'Rocked in the Cradle of the Deep,' 'A Life on the Ocean Wave' and one which men who'd had five or so pints thought seriously about, 'Shepherd of the Hills, I'm Coming Home'. The looks on the faces of people coming down the steps made you overjoyed that they'd braved it and that you'd watched. They all seemed to have a little trouble walking however afterwards and not one looked back with joy on their faces. It was definitely a dare ride. All the other rides were ordinary in comparison.

At the fair your cash was soon separated from you as you tried to double your Feast Money. The 'Roll a Penny' stalls always seemed to be the easiest way of doing it but the stallholder didn't really throw a lot of your money back to you. Then the slot machines beckoned, but there weren't many of those that weren't broken down and or that gave you money back either.

Granddad Bird always came and called for me when the Feast came to visit. He and his wife lived against the Empire cinema at the end of High Street. On one occasion we went straight to the first coconut shy stall where he proceeded to knock all the nuts out of their stands. It was a penny for three balls and the stallholder gave them to you saying, "Hit them on the top to win". But he didn't have to tell Granddad how to win. He must have been a great cricketer when he played for Ardsley as his aim was true every time he threw. He didn't however hit the nut on the top to win. Instead Granddad hit the cup that was holding the nut such a blow that the nut seemed to jump out. Every time he threw it was a coconut and we soon had droves of people following us. But alas, although he gave the coconuts to children following us, he was only allowed three balls at each stall. In a way history was repeating itself, he was blackballed again!

But the Feast only lasted a week and soon life was back to normal, that is until the summer holidays came round. Then, together with Jimmy Sadler and Frank Steel, we spent most of our time in the Hilly Fields again. We usually called at a house on the Park Top first.

Mrs Rollin lived there and she made great herb beer which only cost a penny. We each bought a bottle in turn and then walked down to the top of the clay pit which was halfway down and to the left of the Hilly Fields. Here we sat at the top and unfastened the string which held the cork in our beer bottles. We had, of course, given them a good shake first to shoot them in the air to find out who could get theirs the farthest. After we had slaked our thirsts we either walked down to the Rezzer to see whether we could catch a newt, or walked to the pond.

The pond was halfway up the Hilly, at the side of the path which led down to another field that was called Greenlands. It was quite a time before we found out how the pond kept its depth, until we found the spring that fed it. We had been bird nesting, scouring the ground and looking into bushes.

When we wanted a change of scenery the Greenlands beckoned to us. To the right of the path that ran at the bottom of the field was Lundhill Chapel, which was higher standing than Lundhill Row. Each house had its own privy or toilet comprising of a wooden shed with a plank with 2 holes cut in it. It was called a 'seat of ease' but I it wasn't very easy walking ten yards on a cold winter's morning to get your ease! One door was for getting in and a smaller one was for taking the excrement out, which at the end of each day was covered with ashes. It was emptied each week by 'The Midnight Mechanic' who brought round a horse and cart at night.

At the end of the row was a public house called the Lundhill Tavern, where the miners went to get the coal dust out of their lungs and then on home, to face an irate wife because of a spoilt dinner. It was lovely to walk along that leafy lane and to hear the birds singing. On more than one occasion as we walked we would meet a lady carrying a basket with a blanket in it. Everyone seemed to know her and she had been given the nickname 'Mrs Tuppence'. She was not a lady of the night but rather of the afternoon, and seemed to have a gentleman-friend in every hedge bottom. On one occasion we saw her with a fella in the hedge that ran along side the road. When we asked what they were doing they shouted back that they were black-berrying. That of course we didn't believe so we shouted after her, but she put us to flight saying in a well-modulated voice, "Line up at the side of the path and have your money ready boys." We disappeared like chaff before the wind, running on towards the Dove and Dearne Canal and the bridge that spanned it.

After we had crossed the bridge there was a path ahead of us which led on down, through the woods, to the Cortonwood Colliery. It was the way that all the workers from the top half of Wombwell went to work and had a story entitled 'The Monarch of The Wood' attached to it. It began like this; Lots of miners who lived at Hoyland or Hoyland Common would take the short cut to work through the wood each day. That is until *The Monarch's* disembodied cry altered their route. The path ran diagonally from the top of Wood Walk and came out at the Wagon Repair Shops. However there were no lamps to light the way, and it could often be treacharous in bad weather due to the steepness of the climb. It put people off going to work that way when they heard his cry of "I am the Monarch of the wood and you are trespassing on my domain. If you don't retrace your steps, I will put you to death most horribly!" Most people travelling that way believed him and started to set off earlier to work, walking down Wood Walk instead to the pit, while others searched the wood in gangs for 'The King' several times but to no avail. He only seemed to visit his 'Kingdom' when people walked the path unaccompanied. This went on for several weeks, even the local Bobbies couldn't catch him.

It was left to a Scotsman to sort him out. He'd recently moved down to Yorkshire in search of a job with his family and had got a house at Hoyland Common. When told that he'd have to walk down the longer route of the road to get to work instead of the short cut path he said, "Och aye, we'll have to see about that." And so he did, going very early one morning into the wood. Quietly he surveyed every tree until he heard in one, from its branches above, the cry of the proclamation. So he told the tree dweller that he'd brought some paraffin and rags as it must be cold up there and was going to make sure he was warm. When 'His Highness' came down rather quickly to make his escape the Scotsman gave him a lump to wear for a crown. He'd brought his Dudley tin with him full of water because he was going to go to work come what may. With one swift blow he made Wombwell Wood common land once more and without a second glance at the one time Ruler, who was lying motionless on the grass, he set off to work. For a long time after that, people who had started attending the hospital wearing a new cap were looked at very suspiciously. But 'The Monarch of The Wood' was never heard of again in Wombwell.

Back at the bridge at Greenland, we would most often turn right instead of walking to the Colliery, which took us along the canal towpath. This is where the horses had once pulled the barges to get coal from the pits or ironwork from the Elsecar Ironworks. We would walk on the towpath alongside the canal, or the Cut as it was known locally, to the point just outside the Cortonwood Basin. There was a square stone on the bank-side where the barges would wait their turn in bygone days to go under a chute to be filled with coal, and was there that I had my final lessons in the art of swimming.

I was initially instructed in the little pool at the Wombwell Baths when I moved up from the Infants school to the Juniors. Mr Tom Kaye was the manager and he and his staff showed us how to get into old car tyres. These were suspended by chains from the ceiling, and we were helped by his staff who used long poles. These poles had big hooks at the ends which just fitted our little bodies and once in the water, it wasn't long before we were 'little frogs in tyres'. The staff used their poles expertly to keep our heads out of the water so we didn't empty the water out of the bath. But despite all their efforts they never learnt me to swim, but our Les did.

Leslie went with some pals one Sunday afternoon on a walk to the Basin, and I was allowed to accompany them. I should have smelt a rat then but could only think at the time how good he was allowing me to go with them. One of his friends had a black Labrador who came with us too. What I didn't know was that the dog was also going to be learning to swim.

When we got to the canal it was stripping off time and then every one jumped in, apart from Les, the dog and me. Then, without any warning, Les threw me, followed by the dog into the water. Of course the mutt promptly looked for anything to hold him up, and I was nearest to him. I soon learnt to beat him to the canal bank-side however, and after a few more dumpings, I swam with the best of them.

6. Milk Man

I liked school a lot better when I was in the Juniors. That could have been because of our form teacher who was called Mr Whitham. He was a clever artist and a very kind and soft speaking man. I really tried to paint flowers that looked like flowers for him, but to no avail. Mine always ended up as wet blotches, but he said, "Rome wasn't built in a day". I thought privately that my hands had been made for hard work and not painting pretty pictures. How right I was.

English was my best subject and Maths my worst. I could never understand how knowing the length of time it took for a bath to empty, when given the diameter of the hole it was leaking from, would that help me in later life. I failed to pass the 'Scholarship' and so I just went on to the Middle School. It was around this time that I joined Henry Ives, who's brother, Ted, was Head Cowman at Harry Charlesworth's Farm. I helped Henry to deliver milk from an old white horse-drawn ambulance, which Harry had bought from Cortonwood Colliery. He'd bought it when the Ambulance Room decided to move with the times and to take injured men to hospital by motorised transport.

So I was up with the lark, called on Henry and walked down to the Farm. It wasn't long after that before Harry bought a new pony for the milk float. It appeared that this horse had been working at a circus and didn't take to pulling the float at first. So I was given the job of holding her bridle and stopping at places when required. Trixie was a piebald mare and it wasn't long before we understood one another. It did help to cement our friendship by me feeding her my mother's apples from her fruit bowl. Trixie was kept in a field next to the Hilly Fields so, instead of collecting Henry, I collected Trixie. After all the training time, which consisted of me holding her bridle and telling her "Whoa!" when it was time to stop, we got to know one another very well. She especially liked me when it was 'reward time' and she got her apple.

When I appeared in the morning on top of her field wall and shouted her, she came up at a trot and got an apple for her trouble. Gradually by stroking and petting her I got her to let me slip off the wall and on to her back. She'd definitely been ridden before but as she had no bridle I had to hold on to her mane. My legs were just long enough for me to get a grip on her belly and when I told her to "Giddup!" off she went at a trot. We had several practices like this until it was time for me to meet Henry to go and pick up Trixie's bridle at the farm.

This went on for a while until one day I said to Henry, "Why don't I fetch Trixie by myself?" He answered with a grin, "You can try, as it will save me a walk in the morning." So that day when we went home, I took the bridle and the short reins with me and hung it up in the coalhouse. Next morning, complete with apples and bridle I arrived at Trixie's field and in no time at all had her geared up. By this time she was used to me riding her but now I had control with the bridle. The only thing missing was a saddle but it made no difference as we'd never had one in practice either.

The first ride we had was a sedate trot, but after a while it grew to a gallop. We gradually scorned opening the Farm gate, which was a bit awkward for me on horseback. It must have been her circus training that meant she would jump any obstacle whether high or low, but when she did I always made sure my ankles were crossed under her belly. As soon as we got near the Farm however I would slide off her back and walk the rest of the way. I'm sure she enjoyed our morning rides just as much as I did. As for Henry Ives, he said he was mystified as to how fast we'd been that first morning, but I was sure he knew what we were doing. Even if he did, he never said anything. Somebody else however, did.

One morning, after I'd had my ride and was walking Trixie back to the stockyard, a familiar figure was waiting for me. It was Harry Charlesworth who promptly stopped me from taking the milk out. He said, " I can't have anybody riding my horse who isn't employed by me and so isn't insured against any accidents." And that was that. I did miss riding Trixie, although it was nice staying in bed in the morning rather than getting up to walk to the fields.

But life is all about change and after that golden summer came the colder climate of Wombwell Modern School. I didn't have far to go to get there with Dennis Ravenhill, one of my pals who lived at the end of our street. I met him when he galloped past on his imaginary steed when we were very young. So one day, I shot out of our gate and ambushed him, and so began a great friendship. To get to school only took me ten minutes, as I only had to walk on to the end of Jardine Street and go through Dennis' garden. Then I was at the school gates. There were four houses or groups at the school comprising the *Britians, Normans, Saxons* and *Danes*. I was put into The Britains and my form master taught French, which at times when he had his 'French-only-days' became a bit of a bind.

My trouble was also that our Les had been there before me and the teachers took it for granted that I would be as bright as he was. Sadly I soon proved them wrong. The Science Master's name was Mr Grundy and he was built like a wrestler. He was a very accomplished man, who not only seemed to have eyes in the back of his head but also an unerring aim. He was able to tell not only who had been talking when he'd been at the blackboard but could also hit that person, usually on his head, with whatever he was using at that moment, either chalk or eraser. One day we were talking about the properties of oxygen and he was writing them up on his blackboard. But of course I knew all about it, so decided to open my desk to see if I could find something to suck. The next thing I remember was a violent blow to my ear.

All I could think was "Thank goodness he was using chalk." Then he asked me questions such as how you got oxygen from quicksilver. He was mildly surprised when I told him the right answers. Leslie was the next topic of conversation; what was he doing these days and which College was he at. A look of dismay came over his face when I told him that Leslie was working in the Fitting Shop at Cortonwood Colliery. I heard him say, half to himself, "What a waste." But Mr Grundy taught me something that day. It was 'Don't mess about with a crack-marksman.' and I never did again.

The Woodwork teacher was called Willy Welstead and he wasn't just any old wood butcher. He was infact a skilled joiner, who knew all manner of joining pieces of wood. He also showed me how to make a knife box down to the fitting of the green baize in the bottom, which became one of my mother's greatest possessions. Our Metalwork teacher was called Mr Atherton who taught the favourite of my subjects.

In those days I would go to the Hilly Fields with my friends and we would make a camp and a fireplace with bricks. Well, that's what the cowboys did on the pictures, so we followed their example. It's a wonder that we didn't set all the Hillys on fire, but we never did. It was my job to light the fire when all the members of the gang had brought grass and sticks. Everybody in their turn brought a match to light it and sometimes it took a bit of coaxing to get it to burn. I had to blow it into life more often than not, and so they christened me 'The Blower'. So when I first went into the metalwork class after waiting in a line outside the door, the Forge at the end of the workshop took my eye. In time it was my job again to make the fire. It was fuelled by coke and I used to love the acrid smell of it when it was burning.

In Metalwork you decided what you'd like to make and then had a word with Mr Atherton who would put you on the right track. I can always remember the first thing I made, it was a toasting fork forged out of steel. My mother was still using it when I got married, but I had a lot of trouble with my attempt at a fish slice. It was made out of aluminium and I could never seem to get the slice in line with the handle. However I took my attempt home and my mother used it fondly for a while, that is until she became fed up of dropping pie off the precariously balanced slice.

7. Work

I had reached the age of fourteen during the summer holiday of 1938 when my Dad told me that he'd arranged for me to see Mr Fowler. I asked who Mr Fowler was and was told that he was the Engine-Wright at Cortonwood Colliery who was in charge of all the surface workers. I knew the way to the pit as I'd been before when taking messages to Dad, but I was always careful of the shunting engines as soon as I got in the pit yard. They were fascinating but very noisy, comprising two saddle tank engines, one called 'Doris' and the other 'Leslie'. They were never still, keeping everything moving. I knew where everything was too as several times my Dad had wangled me trips on one of the home-coal lorries with Joe Whalin which earned me a bit of pocket money.

My job was to go for the ride and to take the coal notes to the houses while Joe tipped the coal on to the pavement. Firstly we'd had to go to the sidings of the pit where the coal was poured into the lorry, one ton to each compartment, and then we'd go to the Full Weight. This was a cast iron bed outside a brick built building which contained a huge weighing machine and its operator. Joe drove the lorry on to the weigh bed and the weigh man made sure that its load was correct and then wrote the delivery notes out for him. There was a big heap of coal outside the door to be unloaded on to or to be loaded on to our load to make it correct. It was a thirsty job and I had to go to the chemical side of the Colliery where there was a water tap to fill our two bottles. Joe would drop me off at 4 o'clock in the evening and my mother would always say, "Which seam have you been working down today?" because I was so black with coal dust.

The office block, where all the management had their offices, was in the centre of the yard, and that's where I had my interview with Mr Tom Fowler. He was a tall, thin faced man with a small moustache, but a twinkle in his eye stopped all my worries. "How's your Dad keeping? Well I hope?" he enquired. He had a small office and sat behind a huge desk which seemed to fill most of it. He bid me sit down in the chair opposite and asked me what trade I would like to be apprenticed to. Well I had always been fascinated with electricity at school, so I said, "Mr Fowler, please is there a vacancy in the Electricians' Shop?"

He replied, "I'm sorry, I've just set two lads on for that position this week. But I can offer you an apprenticeship in either the Joinery Shop or the Blacksmiths', whichever you'd like." Well I've always liked the smell of wood but I couldn't see me butchering grain as a trade. So I decided on being a Blacksmith and thanked Mr Fowler who told me when I could begin working. Thinking, "Well, I'm off to a good start. At least I know how to light a fire!" I was then off over the fields to tell my family of my new trade. My Dad had already told me that if I wanted to work as an apprentice bricklayer then I could work for a Wombwell builder called Johnson's. But, after considering that builders got laid off in very bad weather and worked in the cold for most of the rest of the time, I thanked him but said I'd rather work at Cortonwood with our Les.

Then the day dawned when my sister, Hilda, went on a shopping spree on Wombwell High Street, all for me. We got most of our purchases from a shop called Scarrot's. Hilda worked her way up; first working boots, then socks, two pairs of bib and brace overalls and then two shirts. Finally she purchased my very own working cap, a sugar and tea tin and an enamelled tea can to brew up in.

When I first started work I was on what was called the day shift. On the very first morning I remember lying anxiously in bed waiting for 'The Buzzer' to go. The Buzzer, which had once been a ship's siren so I was informed, was blown from the Compressor House to wake you and get you up for work. All the Collieries round our area had Buzzers with different notes so everyone knew which one was blowing. If it didn't blow at its usual time it meant there was no work that day. We had to be up at 5 o'clock, have a bite of breakfast and be out of the house for half past. 'We' comprised Dad, Les and me. Our Hilda got up with us the first week to get me used to things but it wasn't long before I did. The weather at that time of the morning was usually cool but as we had to climb a hill to get to the top of the Hillys we were warm in no time at all.

Everybody who was going to work met together and told each other half hearted good mornings, and from then on it was all down hill with only the clatter of hob nailed boots to accompany us. The path down the hill had only one gas lamp that was situated against the pond halfway down it. I suppose it had been put in by the Council to stop us falling in to it on foggy mornings. At the bottom of the hill we then turned left and walked past the Lundhill Rows Pig Sties, across Gypsy Lane and on to Greenland. This was a lovely leafy lane in summer, but in autumn as it was at the bottom of a valley, dense fog blotted everything out, including the path which made it very dangerous. My Dad told me as we walked along that when it was really foggy, men lost the path and would shout "Lost!" When that happened, everyone would stop, stand still and one person on the path would shout "Over Here!" He kept this shouting up until the lost sheep came back in to the fold, cautiously, because he knew very well that the Dove and Dearne Canal was waiting nearby with its icy embrace to enfold him.

It wasn't long before we were crossing the wooden bridge which spanned the canal to the 'Thump, Thump, Thump' of the sound of the

Colliery air compressor. Then it was just a matter of walking down a little path and we were in the Colliery yard, although we had to stride over some railway lines before getting to the Time Office. The Timekeeper had already put my timecard in the rack and showed me how to clock on at the start of my shift and off at the end. Then Les walked me across the pit yard, pointing out the Buzzer, which sat on the main steam pipe. He explained that this took superheated steam to the Winding Engines, adding, "That's what got us up!"

The Blacksmiths' Shop and the Fitting Shops were housed in the same long building, portioned by a wall in the middle. To gain entrance to either Shop when you were inside, was a small steel door built into it. From the outside there was a big wooden door painted green in the middle of each external wall. When we walked into the Blacksmiths' Shop we'd arrived early and there was no one to welcome us. Les walked me to a corner and left me sitting on a big toolbox saying, "Someone will come soon."

So I sat there on the box, swinging my new boots, taking stock of my surroundings. It was a very high building with a long ventilator built into the roof. 'That would be to let the fumes out.' I thought, remembering my school metalwork days. Les had left me at the Atmores' Hearth, which was at the right hand corner of the Shop. There were four more hearths in the building and besides each was an anvil sitting on a block of wood. There was also a half-ton steam hammer in the centre of the Shop, accompanied by a guillotine or punching machine and a grinding machine. These last two machines were driven by a line shaft, which extended from the Fitting Shop through the dividing wall and ran along the top of the wall inside the Shop. All the machines there were driven by belts and pulleys, which got their motion from the big electric motor in the Fitting Shop.

The first person to arrive on the scene was a bright, cheery young man who introduced himself as Jack and told me that he was the youngest member of the Atmore family. He said that his father was the Foreman and I'd better call him 'Mister'. Then there was Young Joe, who was second in command, and Tom. They were both Blacksmiths. In dribs and drabs the rest of the Blacksmiths and Strikers came into the Shop and went to their respective hearths. They sat on big wooden toolboxes which were on the side of fire.

I wondered how they made the fires and asked Jack, who was raking his dead fire out of the hearth. After asking his Dad if he could, he got his shovel and took me out of the Shop by a small door at the end of it which I hadn't noticed. "We get the fire from the boilers," he said, as we walked behind a row of wooden wagons until we came to a gap in between them where men were wheeling barrows full of steaming ashes up a ramp. They had quite a distance to travel before the ramp appeared, and then had to push the barrows on to a platform which stood above another row of empty wagons. This is where the ashes were tipped and the Barrowmen could then heave a sigh of relief and set off back on their return journey. We went through the space between the wagons and saw a sight that could have come straight out of Dante's Inferno. There were men were in another set of wagons, shovelling what looked like dried black mud out of the side doors. "That's called slurry," Jack said, "It's made in 'The Washer' from a coal dust and water mixture."

They threw it behind where other men who used long handled shovels to feed it into the white-hot mouths of a long line of Lancashire boilers. Each boiler had two furnace doors in its end and two water gauges with a steam pressure clock over them. In reality there were two boilers in one and it each had its number painted in white on its faceplate. The Stoker, who had to feed four of these boilers, was a very busy man. He had to make sure that all the water gauges were up to a certain level, adding water when required by opening a valve. He also had to use a long handled rake in order to keep the fires drawing and to pull the 'clinker' out, which was the residue from the slurry. Then he pulled all the ash from under the fire for his mate, the wheelbarrow man, to cool with a hosepipe before taking it up the ramp. I don't know what they got paid but, to my mind, they earned every penny. All that the steam pressure, I was told, had to be kept to a certain level when the Winders were drawing coal.

The nearest Stoker said "Good Morning" to Jack, opened the firebox door and raked some fire out on to the floor, from which Jack took a shovelful. Then we retraced our steps back to the Shop, where he put the fire into his hearth, covered it with coke and switched a fan on. Then he opened the slide valve which controlled the blast and in no time at all the fire was blazing merrily.

Old Joe Atmore then came across to me and said, "What's your name lad?" so I told him. He then suggested that I should go with Jack who would show me everything I needed to see. Before we had left for our tour all the Strikers from the other hearths came with their shovels to get red hot cokes from Jack's fire, and in no time at all, every fire in the Shop was lit.

8. The Tour

First of all we went down our Shop to the steel door in the dividing wall, which led into the Fitting and Machine Shop. The left hand side was filled with various belt driven machines spaced out, stretching up to the outside wall. The right side consisted of rows of wooden benches, complete with steel vices fastened to them and on the floor beneath were piles of underground equipment, all in different stages of repair.

On the way through the Shop I saw our Les working at a bench, who told me that I wouldn't go far wrong if I listened to Jack, so I did. We went out of the main door and across to the Compressor House, where air was compressed to a high pressure and then sent by pipes down the pit shafts to the different seams. "All coalmines," Jack explained, "have an explosive gas called 'blackdamp' which comes out of coal seams. When it mixes with air and is ignited by a spark it can cause terrible explosions, often with a great loss of life. That is why, where it is possible, compressed air is used instead of electricity, which sparks easily, to get the coal out of the ground." We then said "Hello" to the man who was in charge of the compressor who showed me the lever which, when pulled, turned everyone's dreams into nightmares. It of course blew 'The Buzzer'.

We walked across the pit yard, under the main steam pipe which went to the Winding Engines. Alongside it was a pipe of the same size, carrying compressed air down each shaft. Our next call was at the Lamp Room where the miners' lamps, both electric and oil, were overhauled. Managers, Under-Managers, Over-Men, Deputies and Shot-Firers all carried oil lamps. They were used to test for the dangerous gas which came out of the bands of coal. As it was lighter than air and had no smell, the only way to find its presence was to use an oil lamp. Its real name was a 'Safety Lamp' which had been invented by Sir Humphrey Davis, who found out that by using fine gauze in the lamp prevented the gas being ignited by the lamp's flame. When held up to the roof of the 'Working', if its flame changed from yellow to blue it meant the gas or 'Blackdamp' was present.

There were three shafts at Cottonwood Colliery, one was called the 'Coking Shaft' which was disused, with no headgear at its mouth at all. The next one was called the 'Parkgate Shaft' which had been sunk in 1872, and then there was the 'Silkstone Shaft' in 1873. We then went to the Stores, which were at the bottom of a wide flight of steps. The miners climbed down these to go into the mine and acsended them when they'd finished work, to go to the Pithead Baths to scrub themselves clean. We said "Hello" next to Mr Barron, who was the storekeeper. The man walked with limp, which had been caused by a fall of rock when he worked down the pit, according to Jack.

A short distance away was the Baths, which I had a look inside and marvelled at the sight of so many bundles of clothing which were on hangers up in the roof. They were held there by clotheslines which ran over pulleys to be fastened to walls and pillars. On the left hand side of the building were white tiled enclosures which ran the whole length of the Baths, with showerheads fitted to the walls. This was where the miners washed themselves clean, with the occasional back scrub from their mates.

When we came from the Baths I asked Jack where the lavatory was. Just outside was a long building. "It's in there," he said, "Just open the door." I opened the door and found it was a much larger version of the middens, which were in between the houses and pigsties on Lundhill Row. The only difference being that there were about twenty oval holes 'of ease' in the planking, in comparison with the four of Lundhill, from which steam arose lazily. Jack said, "You get a Turkish bath at the same time when you go here!" It appeared that the water from the showers was used to drain the waste away. "We don't waste anything here," my guide said with a smile. "I'll show you where the Oil Stores are now."

We walked up to a long row of old buildings which looked as though they'd been used as stables at some time. A man was standing at the door of one of them and his cap and clothes shone like silver. He looked as though he'd been lowered into a vat of oil, pulled out and hung up to dry. My first thought was, "He can't be a smoker or he'd have gone up in flames long since." Jack said to me as we approached, "This is Mr Jack Wadsworth who is in charge of the Oil Stores, where you'll have to come sometimes for things. But he's deaf and dumb. You'll probably have some trouble making him understand what you want. Don't be put off by the faces he pulls or the noises he makes because he's no idiot. He can lip read and if he can't, he's got a pencil and pad to talk to you with. He's known because of his appearance as 'Oily Jack'. With that I said "Hello" to Oily Jack who pulled a face and grunted, which I supposed was a smile and a greeting. He then bent low and beckoned us into his domain.

We went in to a low, ill lit building filled with barrels which stretched as far as the eye could see in all sorts of positions, with big shiny jugs stacked in a line. Then we escaped Oily Joe's lair and went quite a long walk up to the Mortar Mill where I met Charlie Johnson who besides making clay for the shot-firers also made the stone-dust, which was used all through the mine to stop explosions occurring. I suppose it was because of his job but he chewed tobacco ceaselessly, forever spitting. He was a widower who lived at the bottom of Mellor Road with his daughter, Mary.

We called at the Joinery Shop on our way back and, when we did, I knew that I'd made the best choice of jobs. The timber yard, where my Granddad Bird had once worked, was just outside the Joinery Shop and a gang of men were unloading wooden pit props out of railway wagons. They stacked them onto timber trams which stood on tub rails. These ran down to a ramp which led up to the Silkstone Pit Top, where a haulage engine would pull them up the slope. Then they would be sent down the pit shaft to be used to shore up the roof, while the Colliers dug the coal out of the seam. The Parkgate Shaft was also supplied with pit props but, as it was in a different position to the Silkstone Shaft, the timber trams were put on a hoist to get them up to it.

Both the Haulage Engine and the Hoist were operated by compressed air. We looked in at the Electricians' Shop and the 'Powerhouse', where a steam turbine drove a dynamo making electricity for the Colliery and houses that it owned. My guide then said, "We'd better go back to the Shop for our dinner". The kettle was boiling merrily on the hearth fire awaiting us to mash our tea. The elder Joe Atmore asked me what I had thought of everything I'd seen and I told him it had been very interesting. Then he told me that I was going to see the Colliery working. So, after we'd had dinner, me eating my bread and jam and drinking my tea, Jack and I set forth again.

We walked up the pit yard, passing the 'Loco Shed' on our way to the Fan House, which stood at the side of the Parkgate Shaft. The reason being, this was the upcast shaft, where all the bad air which had circulated through all the Colliery's workings, was sucked out by an enormous fan. It had started its life as good air being pulled down the Silkstone Shaft, which was called the downcast shaft. The moving air kept the gas from settling and gave the miners air to breathe. In the Fan House a twin cylindered steam engine drove a huge flywheel using low pressure steam, which had first been used as high pressure steam to drive the Parkgate Winding Engines. It then had exhausted into steam receivers which were at the back of the Winding House to drive the Fan Engine's flywheel. These in turn used cotton ropes which spun the Fan, that was twenty foot in diameter, in its chamber at a frightening speed.

Then Jack said when we came out of the Fan House, "Let's go and see your Dad." So off we went to a flight of wooden steps which changed direction in the middle at a square platform, where you could have a rest if need be. I'd been to see where my Dad worked before. Our Les had showed me, in case my Mum wanted to tell Dad something of importance or take him something he'd forgotten. When we got to the top of the steps we had to open a sliding piece of wood which marked the start of the first air door. Then we had to step inside the space and close the slide. We had to do the same at another air door which was in front of us then. This was because all the air had to be sucked out of the shaft by the fan and anywhere else it could suck air from would lessen the suction. Even the two double-decked Cages which occupied the pit shaft had airtight covers on them to seal the shaft over when they went down. We could hear the wooden boards, which covered the shaft, banging down when we finally got through the air doors.

My Dad, apart from his many other jobs, was the men's Checkweighman. He sat in a little office with another man who I knew to be Mr Sockell, the coal owner's Checkweighman and a very kind man. They had a weighing machine in front of their office and a desk, which had two large ledgers on it, in front of them. When a workman pushed the tub on to the weigh, he called out the number on the 'motty'. This was a cast iron number with a hole in it, fastened to a small hook on the end of the tub by a piece of tarred string. The Colliers who hewed the coal and filled it into the tub had a bundle of 'matties' and used them to mark the tub of coal as theirs. Then the Checkweighmen both recorded the weight of the coal against the man's name for payment and against each other for correct weight in his own ledger.

We then carried on into the Pit, saying "Hello" to every body we passed and following the tubs of coal on their journey. Further along was another arrangement of air doors, but with a longer distance between them so that a number of tubs could be let through. The doors were operated by compressed air. We followed into the open air where they ran on tub rails to a 'Tippler' or cylinder, which was large enough for the tub to fit into. When a man pulled a lever it turned the tub over and emptied it completely for its contents to go into the 'Screens'. The tub then went back round to the empty side of the shaft to be sent back down the pit shaft to be filled again. Each seam had its own Tippler and Screens so that they would be able to fill the customers' orders without any mix up from the other seams.

We followed the coal from the Tippler by walking down some steps from the 'Pit Hill' as it was called, on to the Screens. Wooden coal wagons, each with 'Cortonwood Colliery' painted in white on a red background, ran on sloped railway lines underneath us. When the coal was tippled out from the tub it fell on to a series of steel plates, each with a set of holes in them. The hole size was dependant on what coal the customer had ordered. These plates were shaken mechanically so all the small coal dropped through them to be taken by a rubber belt to the Washery. The rest of the coal was shaken on to a plate belt made of pieces of steel linked together to form an endless belt, which ran to the end of the Screens. There it emptied the lumps of coal into the wagons. Any larger pieces of coal or dirt were taken off the belt by men who stood at the side. The dirt was crushed to make stone-dust and the big pieces of coal were put back on the plate belt when the customer wanted 'large lumps'. Both the Parkgate and Silkstone screens were built in the same way and were ill lit with little or no ventilation. How the 'Screen Hands', as they were called, breathed was beyond my comprehension as, every time the Tippler emptied a tub, coal dust shot out in every direction.

Then we retraced our steps, Jack saying, "I'll show you how the coal gets to the top now. Follow me." We went to the empty side of the Parkgate shaft and saw that the double decked Cage there had just landed. Two men were pushing two empty tubs into full tubs to move them out of the Cage. "The Winder just brought those from the pit bottom," Jack said. We went through another set of air doors and then we were outside in the fresh air. In front of us the Winding House stood. It was a big brick building and from two long slots in its facing wall, one halfway up and the other near its roof, a thick round rope emerged. The rope from both holes went up to and round the winding wheels, which stood on top of the concrete headgear.

Jack explained, "Those ropes are made of a steel called plough shear. It's a steel that's very strong and will bend. The strands that make them are all locked together by the rope-making machine when it's made, to make it unbreakable. They both wind on to a drum inside the winding house, one at the top of the drum and one at its bottom. Then when it revolves, one rope winds on and the other one winds off. Both of these ropes are attached to a chair or Cage and so either one can be moved to anywhere in the shaft depending which way the Winder turns the drum."

He opened the Winding House door and led me down a short flight of steps to the Winding House floor. We'd come to view it because the tubs had stopped running down to the Tippler for some reason so the Winder couldn't 'wind'. Usually no one was allowed to visit the

Winding House when the pit was working Jack said, but the Winder knew we were coming in and so wasn't surprised to see us. He sat on a sturdy wooden chair which was at the side of one of big windows built into the remaining three walls and beckoned us in. Jack introduced him as Mr Joe Wright who said "Hello Frank. I heard that you were coming to visit us from your Dad and I hope that you'll like working with us." With that, he got up from his stool to show me round. There were two levers and a foot brake in front of his perch and he showed me which one controlled the steam to the two big cylinders. One of each lay at the back and side of the Winding Drum. The other one reversed the engine and could be used as a brake, but only when winding coal and Mr Wright told me that the foot brake was used when bringing men out of the pit.

The floor was covered with red tiles and the connecting rods, which were fastened to the Winding Drum's crankshafts at one end and the piston rods at the other, shone like polished silver. The walls were painted light green and all the machinery which could be painted was a darker green, lined with black paint. Everything was spotless.

In front of and to the side of the Winder's stool was a bank of signals which gave the Winder his instructions by sight and sound. He wouldn't move his engine until the correct signals had been given. The Onsetter was the name given to the man who was down the pit at the Parkgate Seam. He was in charge of making sure that the full tubs were safely in the Cage before 'rapping it off'. Both shafts at Cortonwood were sunk to the Silkstone seam depth, but had landings at other seams in their shafts. The Parkgate seam was halfway down the shaft and, as the Cage was a double decker, with two tubs riding on each deck, each had to be moved again after it had first landed and the full tubs had pushed the empty ones out. The reason for this was because there was only one gallery which followed the seam of coal.

The Winder had to have a stop or a bottom to land the Cages on at two different levels so some clever engineer devised the 'Floating Bottom'. It was a sturdy wooden frame made to cover the area of the shaft where the Cages landed, held in position by two steel ropes, one at each end and over pulley wheels went to the other side of the shaft. These ropes were weighted at the other ends with cheese weights to counter balance the weight of the Floating Bottom and, as the Onsetter had a brake to control the pulley wheels, could with the Winder's help put the Floating Bottom and the Cage at both levels.

The signalling apparatus which the Onsetter, who was at the pit bottom, and the Banksman, who was in charge of the Cage at the pit top, was called a 'Rapper'. It was a flameproof signaller which was operated by hand, one at each side of the shaft. The Winder heard a bell ring and a light lit a panel. It was from the Onsetter saying he was ready. Then there were two bells rung, each giving a different sound and another panel lit up - they were from the Banksman. The Winder pushed his reversing lever over and then gave the cylinders a puff of steam that lifted the Cage up off the 'fallers', which were four steel arms that were put under the Cage at each corner. By the Banksman pulling a lever just after it had been brought up from the depths by the Winder, the fallers acted as a base on the pit top just like the Floating Bottom down the pit. The Winder then pulled back the reversing lever, as far as it would go, adding more steam to send the Cage to the Parkgate seam.

The panel of lights showed the Winder just where he was in the shaft and, when he was near the top he stopped the steam pressure and pushed the reversing lever forward to brake the engine. There was a dial on a stand against the engine marked with all the seams that were in the shaft with a finger on it, telling him just how far he was off landing at any time and just to be exact, he had to match a pointer on the edge of the drum with one on the boards that framed it. That mark matching just brought the Cage above the Fallers so the Banksman could get them under the Cage. When the two full tubs had been unloaded from that deck of the Cage the signals came to the Winder as before, first from the Onsetter and then the Banksman, to bring the other deck of the Cage down to be unloaded. And while all this was happening I never saw a wisp of steam anywhere in the Engine House.

Then my guide said it was time to go and look at the other Winding House. We went out of the back door of the building and down some steps to see three large steel cylinders standing at the bottom of them. They received all the low pressure steam which had been used by the Winding Engine to be used again by the Fan Steam Engine. Jack told me on the way to the Silkstone shaft that Joe Wright was a model maker and that he had a big shed at the bottom of his garden where he made working models of the amusements for the Feast and the traction engines which pulled them. He didn't just know how to drive them but knew how to build them too. He was a very clever man.

We passed the Electricians' Shop on the way and then went into the Power House to see high pressure steam drive a big steam turbine, which was coupled up to an equally large dynamo to provide all the Colliery's needs of power and light. The steps that the miners went up to go down in the shaft were at the side of the Power House so that's the way we went, climbing to where they levelled out on Silkstone pit hill. The way into the other Winding House was in a door at the left hand side of it, one hundred yards from the shaft. That's where we were told to wait until the Winder had brought the Cage up to his coal winding mark. All the four full tubs were on the same level in this Cage but were unloaded in just the same way as at the other shaft, with two men pushing empty tubs into the full tubs. However firstly the Banksman had to pull a lever inside the Cage to unfasten the catch which held the tubs safe on the journey up the shaft before they could be pushed out. Then, as before, at the other shaft they were sent down an incline to be weighed by the Checkweighmen and registered in their ledgers before running down on tub rails to be unloaded onto the Screens by the Tippler.

The Silkstone Seam Winding House was laid out exactly as the Parkgate one. The Winder in here however was called Harry Wall who had been a Banksman before learning to wind. He said "Hello" and then we watched him wind coal from the deepest seam. Although both shafts had landings in the walls for all the seams, some had been stripped of all their coal like the 'Barnsley Bed' which was 12 foot thick and didn't need any supports to hold it up. This particular seam came to the surface in Elsecar Wood but it had been worked out there too by coal pickers in various strikes over the years. Incidentally it did have the reputation for being the best domestic coal ever found in the coalfields. The Winding Drum at the Silkstone Shaft however was different. It was in two halves but twinned together and held fast by a large bolt at the middle of its boss which, when loosened, would allow the Cages to draw coal from any of the seams. This was of course, after the Winder had moved the half drums to their marks for the new seam and then the bolt was tightened up again.

Then we were on our travels again, walking from the pit hill down the ramp where all the materials for the pit were pulled up in tubs or trams by a steel rope fastened to the drum of a compressed air operated haulage engine. There was a haulage system used down both pits, where a steel rope ran around a pulley wheel at one end of the workings to another one at the other end, and it went around that one too. It made an endless rope that was powered at one end by a haulage-engine. Tubs were pulled from anywhere in the pit to the pit bottom by using a lashing chain round the rope and coupling it to a number of tubs by the end link to the drawbars. Where the coal seam was being worked was too far from the haulage rope for the tubs to be picked up, pit ponies were used to pull them on tub rails to the main haulage-way. Two signal wires ran alongside the haulage rope to be used by the haulage lads to have the engine driver stop or start, as was required, by them by coupling the wires together with a knife or a piece of metal.

Then we went to the Saddler's Shop where everything that was needed by the pit ponies was made. His Shop was housed in the old Powerhouse which was reached by a long flight of stone step. It seemed to be stocked simply with sheets and sheets of leather and you couldn't see the wall above his long bench for knives and hammers.

Then we stopped to look in a large building against the Lamp Room and the Offices, where water was being mixed with chemicals in big tanks before it went into the boilers. Jack said it was done to stop the boilers becoming filled with limestone when the water was boiled. I knew where the office block was as that had been my first port of call. What I didn't know was that the two concrete shapes against the Offices was where all the steam went to after it had been used. It changed back to water there before running into a pond or 'lagoon' as they called it. Then it was pumped to the mixing tanks to begin its journey once again. The pipes took it underground to where the tall brick chimney stood like a sentinel guarding the boilers. Here it produced the draught to keep the boiler fires glowing and get rid of the smoke.

Finally we visited the Bricklayers' Cabin and met Cyril Dale who was the bricklayer and his little mate. Albert was a Lancastrian who had just one tooth in his head and on his feet he wore brass toe-tipped clogs. Then my tour was over. Jack said, "We'll just get back in time to put the bucket on the fire with a bit of luck". And that's what we did. He showed me a tap against the wall inside the Shop where I filled it with water. Then we went to his hearth and put it on the fire to warm it up for everybody to wash their hands in when the shift was over. I was shown how to put the bucket into its stand and where to get the box of soft soap out of a cupboard. Everybody used it to get their hands free from the grease of the day. Then it was just a matter of walking across the railway lines to the time office. The Buzzer blew its mournful note to clock off and so we put our best foot forward to walk home.

9. The Union

Those workmen who had jobs on the surface all came home at the same time apart from my Dad who worked the 'Colliers' Time' and came home earlier than us. He had been voted into his job by a Colliers' ballot, whilst Horace Sokell had worked in the wages department before being appointed as a Checkweighman. They were the best of friends and, as far as I knew, worked well together. Friday was the only day Dad didn't go home early as he stayed and took contributions from the workmen who were in the Yorkshire Miners' Union before or after they came off shift. He shared a 'Union Box', which was a brick built building adjoining the Platelayers' Cabin with Joe Smith, who was aptly named as he was a Blacksmith. He was also the Secretary of the 'General and Municipical Workers' which was the Surface Workers' Union. Naturally, I was to belonged to the Miners' Union. There were two big windows in the 'Box', one for each Union, through which the men paid their dues. Each with his Union card to be marked down as paid in a big ledger. (I bet Father was fed up to his back teeth with ledgers!)

On Friday night his Treasurer, a man called Tommy Chipchase who lived on the top of the Hilly Fields, joined him at our living room table. Father would bring his book home from the pit and then relayed to Tommy who had paid and who was off sick. This was then recorded in Tommy's ledger, which in turn was sent to the Miners' Offices in Barnsley for them to keep a finger on the monetary pulse. Usually, when they'd finished their clerking, they would walk down to the Reform Club, which was at the bottom of Hough Lane, to celebrate a job well done. They'd have a couple of pints and a game of billiards. We had a three quarter size billiard table at home, which we kept behind the settee against the wall. Father had acquired it from the Reform when they had purchased a new one, along with all its accessories including the billiard cues.

My mother used one of these to root us young ones out from under the kitchen table if we'd hidden there after doing something wrong. Jip our dog, who was a small smooth haired terrier, always joined us too. If he hadn't been quick enough to see the cue coming Jip was used as a shield to keep us from all harm. But if he did see it in time and got out of the way and ran, guess who was the first reserve. Jip, although small in size had a heart as big as a lion and defended his territory ferociously against dogs who were a lot bigger than he was. The one thing that put him to flight however was the billiard cue, handled so cleverly by my Mum!

Father used our sitting room, which Mum kept shining like a new pin, for his Union members to air their grievances to him on Sunday mornings. He would usually have Tommy Chipchase with him. As well as cleaning, Mother had to provide refreshments when required for those impromptu meetings. I was never invited in so I could only guess that they talked things over and decided what steps to take in each case.

Then Father would see the management later in the week with a committee member to see if he could get things settled to the requirements of both parties. If not it was brought to the Guide Post public house where a Union meeting was held every fortnight. There, in front of a full committee and other Union members, all the pros and cons of the matter in hand would be reviewed and decisions made as to what steps would have to be taken in the case. However, in some cases when it couldn't be solved locally, the problem would be 'passed to Barnsley' as the Miners' Union Offices were coloquially called.

There was another man who was a regular caller at 21 Jardine Street on Sunday mornings. His name was Joshua Hudson and he had been voted by the workmen to be their Safety Inspector. He was a Collier by profession and worked at that job, but was called to any accidents which occurred at the Colliery to represent the workmen. A smartly dressed man, he always held himself extremely erect and wore a bowler hat. He was also a very talented naturalist. What he didn't know about flora and fauna wasn't worth knowing. He, with his brother William, lodged in Wombwell on Roebuck Street with a family called the Robinsons. William worked in the timber-yard with my Granddad Bird. The coal owners of course, were represented by the Mines and Quarries Inspector, but that didn't give them the edge in any way when Joshua was around.

I got to know the Robinsons as my Dad sometimes sent me with a message for Joss, as everybody knew him as. Alan Robinson, the eldest son, had a B.S.A. air rifle which I loved to fire. Alan also had a passing fancy for Lillian my youngest sister, but I'm afraid it was a case of unrequited love as far as he was concerned. He begged me to get her to go to the Empire with him, which I did. But she made one stipulation before she would go. I would have to sit between them in the pictures. And so that's what happened, with Alan footing the bill. I was sorry they didn't do it again as I could have got used to being a chaperone regularly. I could never however understand how a clever lad like Alan could be interested in somebody who didn't like newts for the life of me. I used to love going to the pictures but not as much as reading, even though my love of learning at times used to get me into trouble.

10. Bright Ideas

There was one day when my Uncle Frank Clarke came visiting us. He lived in Wombwell so didn't have to come far to the pit and as he came along he saw smoke coming out of the coal house grate. This was about five feet up from the path where you shovelled the coal. He couldn't believe his eyes when he opened the door and found a fire going on top of the coal. It was blazing merrily with three black-faced boys adding coal on to it, namely, Jimmy Sadler, Frank Steel and myself. The reason we were in this position was because I'd read how the Romans, who I thought were a very clever lot, had heated their houses up by having a fire in a space built in the side of the house and the heat conducted through a space in the walls. So I thought I'd see if it would work at our house and save everybody a lot of trouble.

Uncle Frank didn't have time for explanations though. He just hauled us out of our 'Roman heating-house' by our ears, adding some new words to our vocabularies which, when we re-aired them in our households, brought on a horrified silence then a beating, followed by a warning what would happen if we used the expletatives again. Uncle Frank then dug out the live coals, mumbling that he could think of easier ways of committing suicide, while we made ourselves scarce.

Another time, after reading Treasure Island, I thought that burying something really expensive would be like living in the days of the Spanish Main. But what had I got that would be like treasure? Nothing, but I knew who had some treasure. So Father's gold watch disappeared into the cabbage patch, luckily to reappear later when the man who had planted the garden found it, much to Dad's surprise as he had never had time to go in the garden. I could only think that I was very lucky that *Kidnapped* came into my hands much later in my life, for everybody concerned.

Uncle Frank, who was my Mother's brother, lived on King's Road with his wife Minnie. He was the Head Rope-Splicer at Cortonwood and a big man, built like a boulder. One of his favourite pasttimes was to come up to our house to play cards. We played Pontoon usually and Uncle Frank took risks that no one else would do. He always said life wouldn't be worth living if you didn't take a chance, and then usually lost! Then he'd pick his flat cap up from the table and give the table a smack to relive his feelings, laugh at his antics and be ready for the next hand. When I was at school, every Friday at home time my first job was to go round to Auntie Minnie's to do her errands, for which she'd reward me with a penny, whether I did any or not. She was a very small quiet lady, the exact opposite of Uncle Frank. Minnie had been a widow before meeting my uncle, but they do say opposites attract.

Personally as a boy, I never had much time for the opposite sex. To me they were excess baggage and always wanted their own way. I remember once, while in the company of a 'fair damsel' at the bottom of the Hilly Fields, undertaking an instruction in the art of house building. So we gathered bricks, (she supervising of course,) and then had me laying them to represent the outlines of the outside and inside walls. The last brick laid finished the bedroom wall. Then she showed me where the bed was and lying down, instructed me to lie down by her side telling me she was tired and I was to keep still. We would have been about eight years old at the time and she needn't have worried about me keeping still. I was as quiet as any mouse could ever be. But I did wonder if all girls had this house-building trait instilled into them. After telling her that I'd actually just seen a mouse, I marvelled at the speed that she shot up on to her feet for somebody who'd been so tired. Then, while she wrapped her dress tightly around her knees, I made good my escape.

It was ironic but it was at that very spot, where that young lady showed me how to build a house, my sister had taken me to see houses or rather shelters that had really been built to keep the weather out. It was just after the 1926 strike and I must have been just over two years old. The builders were all families who had been turned out of their houses on Lundhill Row. The reason given of course was they couldn't pay their rent because they were on strike. The situation had been brought about by the Coal Owners who, on behalf of their shareholders, had decided to cut the miners' wages. The builders of these shelters hadn't used bricks, as the only materials they had were clothes props and sheets of various colours. To my young eyes it was a marvellous sight to see, the biggest multi-coloured tent in existence, as everybody had pitched on to each other. Our Gwen had to pull me away with threats of never bringing me to see it again if I didn't come home that second. How long this situation went on I have no idea but I never saw the tent again.

Help in some form did come however for these poor unfortunates who lived in mining areas caught up in the strike from all over England. My sisters were given the task of sorting out donated shoes from big wicker baskets which had been sent to our house. They were sorted into pairs and sizes before they were sent to the Guidepost for distribution. My Father had given both girls strict instructions that they weren't to keep any as they were for people who hadn't got any shoes at all. A difficult undertaking for two teenage girls!

As we walked down to work my Dad used to tell me things that would help me as I went through life. He said, "In this life you'll meet all kinds of people; good, bad and indifferent. Treat them all as you find them." He also told me a story about Lady Astor who, when told of the start of the strike in 1926 said, "What are the earthworms wanting now?" which really enraged me. I wished with all my heart that she could have been taken from the House of Lords, stripped of all her pompous regalia and made to work in the dark, filthy conditions in which her so called 'earthworms' earned their paltry wages. Then she would know what they were wanting now.

11. A Living Wage

I gradually got used to getting up early when the Buzzer blew its mournful bellow, meeting my workmates and getting our jobs to do. The first thing I had to do now was to fetch the fire from the boilers. The slurry, which was used to feed the boiler fires, was brought into the workshop in wagons and when they were empty had to be pulled out from in front of the Lancashire boilers. A new set of full ones had to be put in their place, but a gap had to be left in the line of wagons for the barrow men to take the ashes out. When this was going to happen the 'Shunter', who coupled the wagons up, had to be at the gap to stop people from going in between them when the shunting engine pushed the wagons together. I'd got into doing this job easily without any bother at all until one morning when I was in the middle of the gap and heard the clang of buffers. This was the shunting engine banging into the end of the empty slurry wagons.

Instinctively I threw myself down in between the tracks, my shovel at my side. Hearing the buffers bang together over my head and hoping no one had seen anything, I slipped out between the wagon wheels and waited until the empty wagons had been pulled out and got my shovelful of fire. Someone must have seen what had happened though because later that day I was told to go to the Fitting Shop. I was instructed to find the Shop Labourer and to ask him for some paraffin waste to light the fire with which, I thought, was a safer and easier method for everyone, especially me.

I still went to the Atmores' Hearth to start my working day which consisted mainly of running errands, some of which were authentic, but the buckets of compressed air and left handed spanners I found were not. It was part of the job experience of the time. Some people were good to you when you went finding things that were non-existent and others were not, sending you on to somebody else. It did one good thing although, you found out where every place at the Colliery was. We had our dinner or 'snap' as it was called, at ten in the morning. It was my job to make the tea for everyone in our corner and, as it only lasted thirty minutes it didn't leave me a lot of time to get mine. So I started to have my break in the Bricklayers' Cabin which was just outside the end of our Shop, having had made friends with 'Little Albert'. I would always get him to make my tea!

I also learnt a lot from the people who sat on the planks placed against the wall which were lifted up by bricks to a nice sitting position. A huge coal fire sat in the middle of the wall with a mantelpiece made out of a steel plate to keep all the tea cans warm. In the corner was a big heap of coal to keep the fire in. My errands took me often to the Colliery Stores for different things where I handed my requisition to a Mr Barron. It was there that I found out that the reason he limped was because he'd been working as a Collier down the pit when the roof had come down on him. He'd had his case for compensation fought and won by Father and had also been given a job in the stores. He always praised my Dad and said he hoped that I could be at least half the man he was. I knew that I would never be anything like as good as him so after a while I got fed up of hearing it.

I can also remember every Friday, having to go down to the Butchers with a basin for a quarter of roast pork as Dad loved it. While I was down there I would call at the Post Office for a registered envelope. This was to be used to send George Blow his compensation money. Although the money had been won as a lump sum after his accident, he had bought a pig farm in Lincolnshire with half and the rest he allowed my Father to send in installments. Then I had to take it back down to have it registered before it was sent on to the wilds of Lincolnshire. I can still see the address now, written in Dad's copperplate writing;

Geo Blow esq.
The Piggeries
Sleaford
Lincolnshire

We saw George every Christmas. He used to arrive two days before Christmas Day at our back door with a big wicker basket on his arm, covered with a white cloth. Inside would be twenty large pork pies, the tastiest I've ever had in my life. Round where we lived nobody bought a pork pie at Christmas time and everybody blessed George Blow after they'd tasted them.

When I'd gotten used to fetching things for everybody from everywhere in the Blacksmiths' Shop, I was given a job sharpening 'Cutter Picks'. This was at the bottom end of the Shop, working with a man who'd only got one eye. He had lost his eye when he was using a hammer and chisel to cut the legs off a cotter-pin. One of the legs flew into his eye and it unfortunately couldn't be saved. These 'Cutter Picks' were used in a machine that cut a six-foot horizontal groove into the face of the seam of coal. Then holes were bored above it by men using the same length of drills. They were followed by the shot-firers, who had learnt their trade in the 'Mining and Quarrying Department' which was situated at the top of the King's Road school playground and ran evening classes. This building was surrounded by a thick brick wall and had a roof which was composed of all different types of tiles. This was no doubt as a result of too rich a mixture being used when testing out their skills of explosions!

Anyway, the shot-firers followed on behind the borers pushing cartridges of blasting powder to the bottom of the drilled holes, once they had spiked the end of the cartridge to take the copper cased detonator. The blasting powder I'd seen being unloaded outside the stores was taken inside to await the journey down the mine to the 'Box Hole'. This was the office from which all orders for running the mine were given. The powder was taken down in the wooden boxes to be stored until required so I suppose that's how the office got the title 'Box Hole'.

Detonators were carried in individual loops separated from each other in a 'det-bag' as it was called. These were made from leather and the two wires which came from each detonator were about six foot long .The powder couldn't be exploded unless it was ignited by the detonator or a spark in a confined space, so the shot-firer used a wooden stick or 'rammer' to put rolls of clay called pills behind the powder and then rammed it tight into the drilled hole. The two shot wires were left dangling outside the coal-face waiting for all the bored holes to be charged and, when this was done, the wires were coupled into a long length of the firing cable. This in turn was coupled to a shot-firing battery, which was a small magneto. The shot-firer kept these on his person at all times. When everything was ready he would unroll the cable to a position well away from the face and shout, "Firing!" This was to tell everyone to take cover, which they did very quickly. Then he turned his magneto key which sent a high tension current to every detonator which, in turn, exploded the black powder and brought a six foot thick piece of coal, (times the height of the seam, times the length of the face,) down on to the Pans in fragments.

These Pans were made out of steel in the shape of troughs thirty inches wide and fourteen foot long. They fitted into each other at each end and were made to move in a shaking movement, which was driven by a Pan Engine. This was quite simply a one cylindered reciprocating machine operated by compressed air. While the Colliers were filling the coal onto the Pans it shook to the end of the face where it was finally loaded into tubs. When this was done pit props and baulks of wood were brought on to the face to prop the roof up by Timber-men using saws, hammers and adzes to fit them into place. Then, after that, the cutting machines came back on the scene and started the cycle all over again, with everyone who was part of it knowing what time to start in the sequence to keep the coal going up the shaft.

All the tools that were used often needed repairing and so they were sent out of the pit on top of the coal in the tubs to be picked up by me from the pit top. This was now my second job of the day. I would set out with my big wooden barrow as soon as I got to work and had got the fires going. When I first wheeled it I thought it weighed a ton, but it sort of grew on me in a very short time. My first journey was up the steps to the air doors on top of Parkgate Shaft.

There were usually three or four bags of cutter picks and never less than two broken lashing chains. Sometimes you'd get seven or eight six-foot boring drills and they'd all need to be negotiated through the air doors and down the steps to the Blacksmiths' Shop. Then, once I'd unloaded my barrow it was off to the bottom of the inclined tub rail track that led up to the Silkstone Shaft pit hill. Then I walked up the steps the Colliers used to get to the pit top and across to the full side of the shaft to see what the tubs had brought up from the depths. Then it was just a matter of carrying whatever had been left back around to the empty side, so called because that was where two men pushed the empty tubs into the full tubs in the Cage when it had arrived at the coal landing.

My job then was to get all the tools into an empty tub and get the haulage engine driver to lower it down the inclined tub track where I took everything out and put it in my barrow. Then it was back to the Shop where I could really start work.

I took all the lashing chains to a man called Ellis Foster whose job it was to repair them, with the help of his Striker who worked at a hearth halfway down the Shop. Then, all the drills went to Cliff Burkill who, with his helper, repaired them at the corner of the Shop against the door into the Machine and Fitting Shop. After that all the bags of cutter picks had to be emptied in turn, the amount noted and the ones that were beyond repair counted so that they could be made good from our stock of new ones. While I'd been bringing the work into the Shop my workmate had lit our furnace ready for heating the cutter picks which needed re forging. It was then my job to sort the ones that needed grinding from the forgers.

We had a small compressed forging hammer operated by a foot pedal, with dyes in the blocks for the picks to be forged back into shape. Once this had been done then they were put into a basket which stood in a tank of whale oil to harden them. Some of the picks, the ones that needed grinding, had been tipped with a very hard alloy called stellite, so hard that a oxy-acetylene torch had to be used to braze it on to the picks. These were used when the coal was very hard. I had a tray at the side of the grinding wheel where I put the picks, from where I put them into a pair of tongs before sharpening them on the belt driven wheel.

It was a noisy corner but you got used to it in time. There was a story of a man who used to work doing that job on his own who used to say that he had sulphur in his 'wrisses' meaning his wrists. Whether or not it was the rattle of the hammer that bemused his mind I don't know, or perhaps it was the repetition of the job, but sadly one day he went missing. When the police came asking questions they said the next step in their investigations would be to dredge the Dove and Dearne Canal. Someone had seen him looking intently into it. Unfortunately the force had lost their dredging irons and would it be too much trouble to make a couple for them. So Ellis Foster obliged and the unfortunate cutter pick sharpener was duly found in the fullness of time against the locks just past the canal basin. While I worked I made a silent prayer that it would always be a two-man job while I worked it.

Joe Smith, who shared my Dad's Union office in the pit yard, had a hearth in the opposite corner of the Shop to the Atmores'. Together with his helper they made crossings out of tub rails. I liked Joe and got on well with him, even though I couldn't always understand what he said, he was Scottish you see. If I didn't comprehend I just smiled and everything went off well. His helper was a different kettle of fish though. He was a grown up bully who seemed to take a malicious delight in twisting my ears whenever he thought no one was looking. I never told anyone about it apart from our Les. We were walking home after work and he had asked about the trails of white in the grime on my cheeks. This was just when we were passing the pond. When I shook my head firmly, he wanted to know if I'd like to check on the temperature of the pond water and, as it was a cold day and knowing he always meant what he said, I told him. Whatever happened I never got to know but he must have said something to Joe Smith's Striker because from the next day he went out of his way to help me in any way he could. Our Les could be a very persuasive person if he put his mind to it, one way or the other.

Joe Smith used to put his newly forged crossings outside of the Shop against the side of the air compressor, having first drawn the shape he wanted to make them to on the floor. We always threw our scraps of bread outside there and I can always remember the day a sparrow hawk who had his 'eyrie' on the tall boiler chimney swooped down so swiftly to take a sparrow that all that marked its passing was a puff of little grey feathers. That's when I thought it's really true when people said 'In life we are in death'. I'd never believed it before but, after witnessing that tragedy, I did.

When all the cutter picks were sharpened it was time to take them back to their respective pits and then I used to come back for the lashing chains. I used to marvel how Ellis Foster could manage to weld the broken chains together, as he'd only two fingers and a thumb on his right hand, which held his welding tongs. Apparently he'd been putting a piece of steel on the bottom face of the steam hammer when the top face came down, resulting in him losing two fingers. But still he welded the chains marvellously, and sweated copiously in doing so.

If I hadn't many chains to take up I'd put a few drills on my barrow, but had to make sure I sent them back down the pit they'd come from. The Blacksmith who repaired the drills was a Farrier as well, and made horseshoes for the ponies which worked down in the Parkgate seam in his spare time. He went down the pit and shoed them in the stables which he said were kept very clean and whitewashed regularly. They were ruled over by a horse keeper called George Ball. George kept a keen eye on the pony drivers to make sure they didn't ill treat their steeds and kept all his ponies in tiptop condition. My Dad swore by George's horse lineament which was George's own concoction, but I didn't think my Mum liked it a lot as it had the most peculiar smell which would linger about you for days, no matter how hard you washed.

12. Avondale and Adolf

The summer before I started work I went on holiday. I always went to Scarborough with my Mum, just the two of us. She'd been ill for a while so we went in Mr Watkiss's car. Mr Watkiss was a staunch friend of Dad's and he was only too happy to take us. Scarborough was the family's favourite resort and I was really looking forward to the holiday. We always stayed on the North Bay at a guesthouse called Avondale where we kept to ourselves and paid for the Cruet. It was just like a home from home, until the second day.

We had just walked back from Peasholme Park, where I'd been paddling a canoe round the island which was in the middle of the park waterway, to arrive back at our lodgings in time to make ourselves presentable for tea. Much to our surprise we found out that we weren't the only guests staying there when coming down, as we had been previously. Where we had been two, now we were three.

Mum and I sat at a table against one of the three bay windows in the dining room for our meals and now, lo and behold, at the table next to ours sat a singularly well-dressed gentleman. He smiled and said, "How do you do?" and "Good afternoon." A well-spoken man I thought, but there was something about him that put me on my guard. The meal proceeded in a dignified silence and all was well with the world until he introduced himself as, horror of horrors, a retired schoolmaster!

"Well!" I thought to myself. Once again my premonitions had turned up trumps but couldn't see how it could interfere with our holiday at all. How wrong I was. Looking back I suppose he thought my Mum was fair game and a widow woman to boot, but I could have been wrong in my supposition. It turned out that I wasn't though because he came to our table and introduced himself further, much to my annoyance. He asked how old I was and which school I went to. He was all ready to set me some sums I thought so I decided to dampen his ardour by asking my mother if she was ready for her after tea walk, to which she replied with a mystified nod. Once outside I pleaded with her that schooldays were for schoolwork and holidays were for enjoying yourselves and, to my mind, the two should never be mixed. However after giving me a lecture about being too outspoken, she seemed to come around to my way of thinking.

As for the schoolmaster, I think he got my message and apart from passing the time of day with us kept to his own table, much to my enjoyment. But alas, Saturday morning soon came round and with it Mr Watkiss, his car and home.

It was about this time that there were rumours of war, with everyone wondering if it would happen and hoping it wouldn't. It was 1938 and I was fourteen years old. Adolf Hitler had hoodwinked everybody he came in contact with and Mr Chamberlain gave us a 'peace in our time' message, while everybody feverishly started preparing for war.

At night I used to watch the searchlight beams which seemed to be stationed around South Yorkshire's main railway marshalling yards at Wath on Dearne. They flickered across the sky in pursuit of an aircraft and, when one found it, all the others fastened onto it making it shine like silver. The anti-aircraft batteries, which were usually stationed in fields, used the plane at the same time for practice but I never saw them. They must have been well camouflaged.

Word got round amongst us youngsters that a searchlight unit was in a field at the side of the Lundhill Tavern so one night I decided to walk down to see them in action. The whole unit seemed to consist of an army lorry with a diesel generator on the back of it, complete with one soldier in charge. When I arrived on the scene he was polishing the lens of a huge searchlight. After saying "Hello" and asking would he mind me watching for a while he said, "You've just come at the right time." He jumped into the cab and beckoned me to come up. "I'll show you how we start it up." He twisted a key and pressed a button on the dashboard and, after a few whines and thumps, the generator sprang into life. He then said, "We'll go outside now." and motioned me to stand behind the Searchlight with him and then pulled a large switch down.

A brilliant light shot out of the lens with a swishing sound. I never knew that light could make a noise but found that it could that night. Then he said, "I'm afraid you'll have to go now as the rest of the unit will be on duty shortly, and you'll be in the way." So I walked back home up the Hillies, stopping occasionally to look back and watch the bright shaft of light scour the heavens, to be joined by others awaiting the elusive planes. I couldn't stop wondering as I walked up the hill, who had picked the place so close to the Pub? Surely it would be all beer and skittles. That is until the wind blew from the nearby sewage farm, then it would be all hands to the gas masks!

Everyone had to go to Wombwell Baths to be fitted with a gas mask, even young babies who were fitted into a cot-like-gas mask. They were to be kept on your person whenever you went out. People usually slung them round their necks in the cardboard boxes which they were kept in. But some people wore tin containers which didn't get flattened when you sat on them. It was a time of change. A pillbox appeared at the entrance to the pit yard from our lane, complete with two slots cut into its sides and a concrete roof. It was made out of a Lancashire boiler and had a hinged door at the back for the Home Guard to get in. This was so he could defend the Colliery against the Germans with broomsticks through the slots! Every Colliery had it's own 'Platoon' but they didn't have any guns to defend anybody. Instead they drill marched very smartly and always turned up for parades. Air raid sirens were appearing on the sides of buildings all over England but many people said knowingly that they would never be used. Little did they know!

Adolf Hitler was still massing troops on other countries' borders and, in some instances, going over them and turning them into the Third Reich. Everybody knew he had to be stopped and so it was England that told him the next time he annexed anybody it would mean war. Whether he thought he'd get away with it I don't know, but on September 1st 1940 Germany invaded Poland. So, on September 3rd Britain, France, Australia and New Zealand declared war on Germany.

Air raid wardens were enrolled and they patrolled their allotted areas at night, religiously making sure everybody's blackout curtains were keeping light in and not letting any out. Then, on orders from above they would take their gas rattles out for an airing to give us a gas mask drill, just to make sure we hadn't left them at home. This was also the time of the Anderson air raid shelter deliveries, when lorries brought sheets of curved corrugated steel to your door. The amount depended on the size of your family. Then everybody found a shovel and proceeded to dig a hole in the back garden big enough to hide it in. I remember one of our Leslie's workmates from the Fitting Shop came to help us, Eddie Crossley. His Dad was the yard Foreman at the pit. I remember the weather was fine and Mum kept us well fortified with drinks and sandwiches and, although our shelter was the biggest one you could have, it didn't seem to take long before we'd got it finished. That was with steps hewn out of the soil down to the entrance.

Eddie Crossley joined the Royal Air Force as soon as he could but hadn't been in very long when he was killed by a German plane strafing his camp in a daylight raid. He was helping to dig in a gun emplacement out on his airfield and that sad incident really brought stark realism about the war to our doorstep.

Lots of young men enlisted in the Forces from the Collieries before the 'Reserved Occupation' became law. Of course men were needed to replace them down the pit. My Dad hadn't got many faults but the one that stood out in my mind was when he volunteered our family. Our Les was the first Fitter to leave the Fitting Shop for underground duties. Father used to say to me, "Never put yourself in a position where people can point a finger at you for doing something wrong." I replied "Well I'll try, but never to my mind is a long time Dad."

Just before the war it was decided by the Colliery owners that all men over seventy years old should be retired. My Granddad was seventy-one at the time and he was one of those who were finished. This was much to the annoyance of the Foreman joiner who was in charge of the timber yard, who lamented that he'd lost 'two good men' when my Granddad had finished from his timber team. Granddad had a house at the top of Hough Lane in Wombwell. His second eldest daughter Lily and her husband, George Boyes lived with him too. She was a schoolteacher and he was a constructional engineer.

I was sometimes sent up on errands to their house, glad to see Granddad but all the time hoping he was on his own. I must been on the plump side because whenever George saw me he would call me 'Charlie Lard' which used to annoy me, but I never let him see it. But I must have been out of sorts one day because when he greeted me with 'Hello Charlie Lard' I replied, 'Hello Silly Bugger'. In my own mind it gave me some satisfaction but also gained me a clip round the ear-hole from my Dad. He told me that he didn't like George overmuch eIther, but accompanied it with the old adage; "Children should be seen and not heard." He also told me that he didn't want to be told that I'd 'blotted my copybook' again ever. I thought to myself, 'The mind is willing but the body weak, but I will try'.

Work took a lot of my time up. I was always working on the day shift and had to until I reached the age of 16. Then I would be able to work different shifts and, finally, I'd be able to go where I'd sent a lot of material down the pit. Everybody had their ears glued to the wireless at this time waiting for news about the war, so all the wireless batteries had to be kept charged. Three batteries were needed to work the wireless if you'd only got coal gas for heat and light like we had at that time. The batteries were a 6-volt wet accumulator, a 9-volt grid bias and a very heavy high-tension battery. You had to have two accumulators, one being charged at your nearest garage while the other one was being used. The other two batteries, being dry ones, lasted a lot longer before needing changing. It was my job to take the accumulators to and from the nearest garage and, if you weren't careful to keep them away from your leg you needed a new pair of trousers and sometimes a trip to the doctors courtesy of the battery acid!

The winter nights were hard to get over as you had only enough money for one trip to the pictures if you 'tipped up', which was the term given to giving all your wage to your mother. Then, she in return, would pay you spending money. This was the unwritten rule in most households which only changed when you got to the age of twenty-one or got engaged to be married.

Youth clubs started up at the beginning of the war but were mainly attached to churches and I didn't have any interest in that direction. I didn't want to be bitten twice. We were fortunate in having a dance hall called 'The Futurist' on the High Street at Wombwell. It was at the bottom of Cemetery Road, but I didn't have any interest in tripping the light fantastic. I did go there on Sunday nights occasionally when 'In Town Tonight' was promoted by the owners. These nights were when the 'Local Talent' were invited onto the stage to entertain. They still had to pay the entrance fee like everyone else but could win a prize of first, second or third depending on the volume of the applause after they'd finished their act. This was judged by the owners but everyone loved it! I never did hear of anyone from there ending up on the 'Silver Screen' or even on the wireless though.

Then, when we came out, we went on to the *Bunny Run;* boys and girls in groups walking along the High Street in the hope of meeting a future mate. Most of the winter nights, weather permitting of course, were spent around the gas lamp just outside our house, where the hilly Mellor Road met the flat Jardine Street. We were a mixed bunch of girls and boys and the game we usually played was Hide and Seek. It usually didn't last very long as somebody would move a dustbin to hide behind and bring an irate householder out to move us on. So then we'd go down Mellor Road and play at *Kick Can* until we were shouted in for bed, weary and sometimes badly bruised, but happy with our lot in life.

It was about this time that a new apprentice came to work in the Blacksmiths' Shop and I was given the job of showing him where everything was, and he took my job on. I left the cutter pick corner and moved across to the other one, against the door into the Fitting Shop where the boring drills were repaired. As the Blacksmith I worked with also shoed the pit ponies, when we'd got all the drills repaired I helped him forge the horseshoes. As I wasn't sixteen though I couldn't go down the pit to help him put them on. When he went down to do this I went with Ellis Foster to the screens at change over time, which was when the Winders stopped winding coal and let the afternoon men down the pit and brought the day men out. We went to change the riddles in the shaker, which was under the tippler as a different size of coal were wanted by the customer, taking spanners and hammers and chisels.

The riddles were bolted on to the shaker frame and usually needed the nuts chopping off the bolts which held the riddles in position. As it was dark and with not a lot of room I would hold the lamp while Ellis chopped them off. He did so with great difficulty as he had only the one thumb and two fingers on his hammer-holding hand. He always carried, 'The Green Un' in his pocket to use on jobs like these. When he missed the chisel head and hit his hand he tore off a piece and after moistening it stuck it on the wound. Then I took the tools gingerly and tried to get our own back on the nut while Ellis recuperated and so between us we got the job done.

I liked working with Ellis as he would tell me stories about the First World War saying that he had enlisted when he was 17 and fought in all the big battles. I thought how unlucky he was, going through all the war without a scratch to come home and have his fingers chopped off by the steam hammer.

13. Birds, Clarkes, Greens and the Great Unknown

While working against the Fitting Shop wall I made an acquaintance with a man called Reg Harvey who worked on one of the lathes. He had been a schoolteacher according to our Les. A very clever man who simply hadn't been able to control a class of children. He lived with his widowed mother in Brampton and was interested in Cricket as Les and I were, and Hilda too. We watched Yorkshire whenever we could and that's when Hilda and Reg met and took a shine to each other at once. It was however another case of unrequited love as Hilda couldn't leave my Mum because she was ill and he was in the same boat with his mother.

Our Harold had played the field with all the local girls and then settled down at last, courting a teacher friend of Auntie Lil's. He was soon to be called up and he joined the Royal Air Force. Gwen went to work at Wath Grammar School and also worked in the Co-operative at Darfield, soon to be joined by Lillian when she left school. Then Gwen was called up and she went into the ATS. Eventually Gwen ended up working in an Army Requisitioning Office in North Wales where she met her husband to be, John Tupman. Then Lillian joined the NAFFI to work in an Army Camp in Derbyshire and then became a postmistress in a Co-operative store when she was demobbed. Leslie continued to work down the pit as a fitter but my Mother knew he could do better for himself and wanted him to go into the police force.

My mother's maiden name was Clarke. Growing up she lived in Rawmarsh and, when only a young girl, her own mother died. Her father, as he had a large family, married a widow woman called Green who also had a family. So my Mum had step-brothers and sisters called Green of whom one step-brother was called Sam. He was in the police force and ended up as an Inspector, so she asked him to get Leslie signing-up papers to join. He'd got everything ready for going when he had a sudden change of heart and decided a life in the force wasn't for him. So he worked down the pit for the rest of his life. But, it was his decision and he made it.

Hilda was the backbone of the family who looked after Mum and the rest of us without complaining about her lot in life. My Mum used to tell me about when she first went in to service, of how she looked in the papers at *Domestic Situations* which were available and then decided which one to go to. She went out into the great unknown accompanied just with her tin trunk to an address somewhere in Keightly as a parlour maid. She wrote home to say that she was all right but said to me that she didn't really like the place or the woman who employed her, but thought she'd stick it out for while as it might get better. The weeks went by and it didn't, and to make things worse, her employer stopped letting her having her half-day off. My mother continued to write home throughout the experience. That set off a chain of events.

My mother had a step-sister called Maria Green who was an outspoken lady against anything that, to her mind, smacked of tyranny. That was especially against anybody near to her. So, when she heard of my Mum's dilemma it wasn't long before she was knocking at the employer's door in Keigthly. My Mum answered the door and Maria told her to pack her trunk as she'd come to take her home. She also informed her to tell the 'Woman of the House' that someone wanted a word with her. It must have been a sight worth seeing; one grim faced woman looking down from her doorstep on an equally grim faced younger one who asked if they hadn't heard the news yet? "What news is that?" she retorted.

"Why William Wilberforce had an Act passed in Parliament forbidding anyone to keep a slave. I thought you didn't know, the way you've been treating my sister. So I've come to acquaint you with the fact. She also wants paying up to and including today's wage before she leaves your compound. Tomorrow a carrier will be calling for her trunk and, if by chance he doesn't get it, I personally will be coming to visit again the day after, complete with a Constable this time. Who, I'm sure, will only be too pleased to hear about your exploits, as he is her brother!"

My mother told me she was paid above what the woman owed her and was sent a glowing testimonial by post. Maria went through the *Domestics Situations* list and vetted them together with my mother until they found one that they both thought would be a good, and so it was. A housemaid was required at the residence of 'Mr Merrill of Merrill's Mills at Bingley', which was in the Colne Valley in North Yorkshire. So, armed with Mum's glowing testimonial they went to check it out and she got the job and said it was just what she'd been looking for.

The household was composed of the mill owner and his two sons. Mum liked their collie dog who gambolled around at her feet when she was hanging the washing out. His name was Rover and he was always bringing her a hedgehog from the fields as a present. There was a gardener who didn't much take to her when she let the birds free from his nets. He spread them in the orchard to kill them when they were full, as they ate the fruit from the trees, but mum gave them a new lease of life when he wasn't looking! But she said he still drove her in the dogcart when she needed to go shopping.

Mr Merrill re-christened mum from Alathea to Annie from the beginning of her service. I suppose he did it just to let her know her place. She did have a bit of trouble at the beginning too with the sons who thought she was fair game. However a word in the master's ear changed all that when he asked them if they'd like to try their luck in the Colonies! One of the overseers from the mill who came to see Mr Merrill on business would have liked to be friendly with her she said. When he came to the kitchen for a drink from the cook he once tried his luck, but she wasn't interested.

14. Ratting

Although my Father had taken an interest in my education he didn't have a lot of time to supervise it. On one occasion he arranged for me to meet a small gentleman outside the Reform Club, which was his usual watering hole. The man came out of the top of Alma Street, which was named after the public house of that name which stood in the middle of the street and was on the opposite side of the road. He came equipped with a small smooth haired terrier that had a spot in the middle of his nose. Naturally he was called Spot. In addition the man had a hessian sack which moved as if it contained snakes. It never kept still, moving up and down as though whatever was inside had St Vitus' Dance!

Coming across the road he said, "Tha must be Tommy's lad. What's thi name?" So I told him and he introduced me to Spot. Then he opened his mysterious bag and two sable coloured ferret heads poked out. They both had pink eyes. "Don't be frightened of them," he said, "Before the day is out you'll be stroking them! All they do is chase rats out of 'oles in walls for Spot to finish them off."

All I could think was "What ever had I done to deserve this?" but added to myself that there must be a good reason for it. There usually was when Father had anything to do with it. Then Jim said to me, for that's what he said his name was, "I hope tha not dressed up as wi goin to rid cemetery wall of its lodgers!" So, off we went on Summer Lane, a valiant band of pest destroyers.

When we got to the beginning of the wall, which was covered in holes, Jim unfastened his jacket and revealed a large sack which he had wrapped around his waist. Giving it to me he said, "Take this up there", pointing to a spot twenty feet away. "While I blog a few 'oles up. Tha'll find Spot 'll follow you", and so he did. While he was 'blogging' he told me what was going to happen. "We're going to put t'ferrets int' wall in their turn. I've starved them a bit to get them int mood. You'll hear where t'rats are with t'scrabbling noise un Spot 'll be frantic, but don't put your ear too near t'hole or youse be wearing a rat for an earring!" Then he motioned to the sacks and explained that they were to put the rats in. "Don't worry, they'll be dead!"

It wasn't long before we had an audience at the other side of the road and I suppose that put some marrow in my backbone. Jim put a ferret in the first hole to start the proceedings and in no time at all it seemed Spot and I heard an ominous rustling and scratching. Spot did his frantic bit while I backed away a bit. But I needn't have worried at all about anything as the dog took charge straight away. A big black rat appeared as though a magician had conjured it up out of the air, but Spot struck it just as quickly. He grabbed it behind its neck and threw it away in one fluid motion and then killed another one in a blink of an eyelid. After that he had to wait a while as the rats must have got an idea what was awaiting them and had gone all shy so he sat back on his haunches and gave a little grin. He must have being saying "I can wait." He was really enjoying himself and it showed.

I, feeling a lot braver, picked the long tailed rats up and put them in the sack. Jim had already told me that I must be sure to count them. It appeared that while we were ratting we working for the Council and as such, got paid a nominal fee. This was two pence a tail which is why I was told I must count the tails.

"All beer money!" Jim said. We must have put a lot of rat families in mourning that day as that first stretch of the wall relinquished about twenty rats. Then we got slowed up a little as the ferret decided to go to sleep on the job. It took about a half hour before he popped his sharp little nose out of one of the holes and Jim promptly put him in a sack on his own. Then we did exactly the same as before, but this time using a fresh ferret.

After three stretches of the wall had been cleared Jim asked me if I'd like to handle the ferrets, but I remembered that old saying 'Discretion is the better part of valour' and replied, "Erm, could I just stroke them this time?" That's what I did and they had a lovely silky feeling to them. However this was not for long as Jim had also showed me their sharp white teeth when he had initially introduced me to them! The sum total of the rats from the length of the wall came to thirty five and Jim seemed to be satisfied with that number saying to me, "It's not the amount that counts but the joy of the chase". He thanked me as we parted and said that he'd see me later. But he must have kept well out of my way because I never saw him again. Looking back though it was an experience that I wouldn't have missed for all the world, in spite of my fears.

15. The Phoney War

It was surprising how time flew while we waited with bated breath during the period of the Phoney War. I was conscripted into the Wombwell Main Home Guard. Why it wasn't the Cortonwood branch I've no idea. It could have been because the 'powers that be' thought that it would be quicker to get hold of me at Jardine Street than from Wombwell Main. I had the shiniest pair of black leather gaiters in the whole troup. My mother really went to town on them with the polish! We learnt how to march in step and how to disguise ourselves as trees. We were also issued with 303 rifles from the last war and were allowed to take them home, although never with bullets, but I suppose we could have used them as clubs in an emergency.

On Sunday mornings we went on route marches and learnt the soldiers' songs from the last war. As a special treat sometimes we marched down to Stairfoot Brickworks complete with five rounds for each of us, carried in the Officers' car of course. There was a great cliff of clay at the Brickworks and we were allowed to use it as a firing range. Some very brave men were in the butts behind high barricades, marking where our shots landed. They did this with red discs on the end of long poles, that is, if they were within their reach. A lot of poles never went up I noticed after we'd fired.

We were about six in number at a time, lying down in a row with either a Sergeant or a Corporal behind us, instructing all the firing movements. I found out that the cartridge cases were what you'd got to watch out for as, when firing, you pulled the rifle's bolt back and the ejected cartridge case from the breech. This rocketed out at a very fast rate and seemed to be attracted by your face. This meant that the solider on the right hand side was peppered with yours while you got shot from the man's on your left. Thankfully no one, to my knowledge, ever got wounded while we were finding out how a rifle worked.

Anthony Eden asked for volunteers in 1940 from the men in reserved occupations aged between seventeen to sixty-five to join the LDV or the Local Defence Volunteers. They were to be on standby to defend the nation while the Army fought abroad, but the initials stood for 'Look, Duck and Vanish' to some local comics. I lied about my age and joined to do my bit and enjoyed it on the whole until weekend working put paid to me turning up for parades.

We went training in Wombwell Wood, which wasn't far away from the Colliery. Learning 'Field Craft' meant keeping your head down below the level of the Fern Fronds whilst moving about like a snake. When we had accomplished this to the satisfaction of our Lieutenant we were formed into two groups. One group started from the top of the wood while the other set off from the bottom, the object being either to capture or disable (or even kill!) our opponents as we were equipped with our trusty 303 rifles. Luckily for all concerned, there were no bullets. Instead, some boffin in the war office had constructed paper crackers which were tied to a long length of string. This was fastened to the sight at the end of your rifle. The other end went to the trigger guard and, by some miracle, when you pulled the string one of the paper crackers exploded - very ingenious.

There were referees stationed in the wood keeping a check on the state of the 'battle'. How they did it I have no idea, but there was no need to worry as it usually ended up as a draw.

We went to the playing field at Wombwell High School to take part in a Field Craft competition and I was unfortunate enough to find a piece of broken glass with my knee. I think that everybody was happy that we'd had an actual casualty apart from me of course, because the full might of the Medical Corps was finally allowed to swing into action. My trouser leg was cut off above the unfortunate knee by a soldier wielding a very sharp clasp knife. I wondered if I might be gaining another wound stripe, but all was well and a dressing was applied just in time for me to be carried by two of my platoon, making a four handed seat to Mr Mayhew's car. This had been rushed to the scene, him being the headmaster of the school. From there I was transported to Dr Dickinson's Surgery who, as well as being our family doctor, was our regimental surgeon too.

Fortunately it was surgery time but I didn't have to wait my turn. I was rushed straight into his consulting room as a casualty-of-war of course. Whereupon the doctor smiled, said hello and told me he'd have to put a few stitches in the wound to pull it together. He did this without hurting me at all. However I wasn't allowed to go back to work and got an army pension book with which to draw money from the Post Office whilst I was limping along. I did hear later on that the headmaster of the school, the day after the incident, had all the pupils out on the playing field picking up anything that looked like a piece of glass.

16. Daun't Pit

Time flashed by and before I knew it I was sixteen and able to go down the pit. I can remember it clear as day, getting into the Cage at the Parkgate Shaft, after collecting our brass-cheques from the underground time office and lamps from the Lamp Room. We had to give our cheques to the Onsetter who was in charge of letting the Cage go down the Pit. In turn he put them in a box, so the number of men down the pit could be found out at any given time. Also the Timekeeper put your name against your cheque number so they could tell who they were.

I went down with the Farrier to the stables to shine him a light and hand him his tools while he shoed the ponies. The Banksman slid a lattice gate up so we could get into the Cage. We were accompanied by three more men, one of whom was an electrician and the other two apprentices. These were the same ones who had just beaten me to the job I wanted, but what will be will be I considered.

We all climbed into the Cage at Cortonwood, carefully negotiating the Jack-catches which held the tubs in the Cage as they were either lowered or raised in the shaft. Then the Banksman let the lattice gate down to keep us safe inside, as the other gate was down at the other side of the Cage. Then he went to his signal rapper and gave three raps to tell all concerned that men were riding.

The first movement up moved my stomach down in the region of my boots. Followed by the drop down when we'd cleared the fallers, it was then rapidly sent to the bottom of my throat. There were hand rails in the top of the Cage to hold on to so I grasped on to one with just one hand just like the other riders, to be in fashion really, but as soon as these dramatic movements happened both hands gripped the rail like grim death.

I soon got used to the downward motion and the way the shaft walls slipped by in the light of our lamps. Then we were at the middle of the shaft where there were openings in the shaft walls which were entrances to seams, and we stopped at one of these. A big hole, over twelve feet high with a wooden platform for the electricians to step on to, was the way into this seam as they were going to work on the seam's telephone wire, with no illumination apart from their lamps. This seam, my Farrier friend told me, was the worked-out Barnsley Bed. It didn't need propping up as other seams did with wooden props, as it had a thick layer of slate above it, keeping the roof where it should be and as level as a billiard table.

The Electrician gave a signal to tell everyone he was off the Cage and the Winder lowered us down to the Parkgate seam, passing the Swallow Wood seam which was lit up and noisy with men shouting to one another. Then we finally arrived at Parkgate, alighting with scarcely a bump on the Floating Bottom. The Onsetter slid the lattice gate open and we were out into a musty smelling atmosphere. There was activity all around us. When we were clear of the Cage the safety gates were swung up by the Onsetter and clipped to the top of it, out of the way of the full tubs which were then pushed in the Cage.

The pit bottom was bigger than I'd thought it would be, with air doors banging when the tubs hit them and the haulage ropes pulling tubs in different directions. We walked along a passage until we came to a well-lit area with whitewashed walls and a smell of horses. We'd arrived at the stables.

I was introduced to the horse keeper George Ball, who said that he knew my father well and asked had I come to learn how to shoe the ponies? Then it was down to work. The Farrier got the pony's leg up and held it between his knees. He cut the horse nails, which were clenched over in the hoof, and with a pair of tongs pulled the worn horseshoe off. The stench was incredible, talk about sweaty feet! It definitely put me off being a Farrier. I was quite happy to supply the illumination and that alone, despite all the entreaties of the Farrier for me to have a go. Also I told him my height stopped me from getting under a pony's belly. So I got a move from that job and went to work in a small Blacksmiths' Shop on the Silkstone Shaft.

17. Wellies and Submarines

The age of steam had come along and the barges were left rotting on the banks of the canals as an offering on the altar of progress. The railways took coal faster to its destination and in greater quantities than ever before. Now, as I was old enough to go on shifts, my life altered and I started going around with young men in a gang on various pursuits. I can remember the first time going to 'The Futurist'. Why we were allowed in I have no idea as it had been a rainy night and most of us were wearing wellies, but nobody seemed to mind. We joined a line of girls to be shown the steps of the 'Palais Glide'. We were actually allowed to put our arms around their waists. What a sight we must have been, kicking our feet up in the air which were encased in rubber boots.

From then on we started to attend 'The Futch', as we called it, regularly and made friends with girls. Once that they found we were harmless they taught us the basic steps of dancing. Some of the boys started going out with girls and took them to the pictures for a start. Some friendships matured and others changed partners after the first date. Usually however, we ended up at the Futch at the end of a Saturday night's session trying to get a last waltz and the opportunity to walk a girl home.

Usually we ended up walking home by ourselves as we were too busy trying to get what was beyond us and missing what was in our grasp. But that all seemed part of growing up in those war years. The enemy bombers started to pay us visits at night and we got used to evacuating to the air raid shelter when the siren played its mournful tune. The Colliery's Buzzer still awoke us in the mornings but if they didn't we knew we could stay in bed as something had stopped the empty coal wagons being delivered to the pit to be filled. It was a lovely feeling, rolling over and having a few more hours in bed.

It was one of these mornings that I decided to go to Sheffield to enlist in the Royal Navy. So, not knowing the bus times, I caught a train at Wombwell main station. I was lucky not having to wait long before one arrived and, before I knew it, I was in Sheffield. Then it was just a matter of asking directions to the Cutlers' Hall where I knew you went to enlist in the Navy.

I walked up to the top of the steps at the entrance and when I got there I was met by a very smart gentleman. He was dressed in a Leading Petty Officers' uniform and wanted to know my business. After telling him I would like to join the Navy, with a view of moving on to submarines, he asked what I did for a living. I was then told that it was out of the question. When I asked why he said, "That job you're doing at the present time is helping the war effort just as much as you being in the Navy." And so that was that.

Feeling miserable I went on my way trying to remember the streets that led me back to the station. I perked up considerably though when I met a girl who lived in Wombwell and then went with her to the pictures. We had fish and chips and, as she knew her way around Sheffield more than I did, (and luckily the times of the trains home too,) we were back in Wombwell in no time at all. As I'd never mentioned why I was in Sheffield to the girl and never told anyone where my trek had taken me, nobody was any the wiser apart from me.

Not too soon after that it appeared that the German Air Force had decided to come out of its shell and had started to bomb the East Coast ports. Then, one Thursday night, it decided to visit Sheffield. I remember it very well. A gang of us had been to the Empire and were walking home when the siren wailed. As we were against King's Road School we went to use their air raid shelter. It was the first time that I'd ever been in it. Underground and in the middle of the schoolyard with steps to be negotiated, the dark and gloom was barely lit by paraffin storm lanterns. All the forms that were scattered about seemed to be in use and, after sitting on the concrete floor until we thought we were part of it, we decided to go and take our chance in the Hilly Fields. The Germans we decided, would have no knowledge of our recreation ground and there would definitely no lights there for them to home on to. So we all trooped out of the shelter much to the annoyance of the Air Raid Warden who was sitting in a comfy armchair against the shelter entrance. I suppose he was only doing his job, and as comfortably as possible too.

As we walked up towards the Hilly Top the sky seemed to fill with what we thought was sheet lightening and as we got to the top of the hill a noise like far away thunder filled the air. At the top though when we looked across to the horizon we saw our first view of the German bombers at work. Fans of brilliant white lit the sky up when the bombs hit Sheffield, followed by dull thuds seconds later. We could only hope and pray that the sharp crack of the anti-aircraft guns which ringed the city could be bringing down the planes that were causing such devastation.

They came again the following Sunday night but nobody, as far as I knew, went up to see them dropping their bombs a second time. We only saw the damage wrought later in the newspapers but it only made us more determined to beat the invaders.

There were alterations at work too. Now that I was older and able to work weekends I saw a lot more of the jobs that had to be done to keep the coal coming out of the pit and the flag which showed to all and sundry, that we'd got our target for the week, flying from the headgear. These jobs had to be done of course when the pit wasn't working, and not too safely in some cases. All the suspension gear, which coupled the Cage to the winding rope, had to be changed every so often. This was accomplished by bringing the empty Cage to the 'low landing', as it was called, which was just below the coal landing. Then they would slide two girders through the Cage. The Winder then lowered the Cage on to them, thus slackening the chains, shackles and detaching hook which had to be replaced with others which had been previously checked for cracks and wear. The removed chains in turn were examined and every piece of equipment was stamped to say which shaft it was used in and what set it belonged to. The examiner had to fill in a *Mines and Quarrying Certificate* to certify that it was safe to be used. One copy was kept in the Colliery files and another was sent to the Mines Inspectorate.

We had to work on top of the Cage to uncouple everything with half of the shaft awaiting, a deep black hole into which someone may make a mistake and end up joining his forefathers. But we always kept half a dozen safety harnesses hanging on the wall, just in case the inspectors came check. We couldn't use them as they were meant to fasten onto the suspension chains we'd just uncoupled. The 'Shaft Men' did use them however when they were working on the shaft walls.

There wasn't a lot of light in the Parkgate low landing as it was lit by just two Bulkhead Lamps on the wall. So all of us who were working on the job had to get an electric lamp from the Lamp Room individually, as they were all numbered and when we took them out a number was written against your name in the lamp-book. While we were working on the chair top uncoupling everything we had to speak to each other in sign language as you couldn't hear anyone speaking because of the noise of the fan which was pulling the bad air up out of the shaft. I can clearly remember putting my lamp on the chair top just for a moment and it being dislodged and sent on its downward journey in the twinkling of an eye. It was recovered from the 'sump', (that was what the bottom of the shaft was called,) by a Shaft Man when it was cleaned out. It had been concertinaed into itself by the fall and certainly put you on your guard, as well as costing you a half-crown for damaging it.

18. British Empire Medal

About this time I was summoned to the office of the man who was in charge of the group of Collieries, of which Cortonwood was one. He was the 'Manager's Manager'. His name was Mr Douthwaite and you spoke his name in hushed tones if ever you talked about him. 'What on earth could I have done?' I thought to myself, climbing up the stairs to the exalted one's office. But I didn't have a lot of time to ponder over this before I was ushered into his presence and was welcomed by a surprisingly young man behind a long desk.

He smiled a welcome and said "Hello Frank." (How did he know my name? Me! The lowest of the low!) "Sit down and make yourself comfortable." So I did, pulling my pit cap off in the same movement. Then he said, "What I'm going to ask you has to be kept in the strictest confidence. You will see why later on, just between you and me." I went cold and thought, 'Whatever he's going to ask me to do, I'm sure I won't be able to do it'. But then he said, "Could you tell me about your Dad? I've been asked to get information about his working life so it can be judged whether or not he could go on this year's Honours List. So, the best person to ask I thought, would be his youngest son. What can you tell me about him?"

"Well." I said. "To tell you the truth I've never seen him much in a father's role as he's always busy helping other people. My mother has had to be both mother and father to me, with the help of my elder sister Hilda. He doesn't spend a lot of time at home but you can always find him in our front room Sunday mornings, listening to men who have grievances at work. He tries to help them in some shape or form, and if he can't then he always puts them in touch with someone who can, he once told me."

I went on, even though I knew I shouldn't. "You'd be surprised where our help comes from. People who you'd never think would care about the working class really do. We have a Barrister who's a household name giving his services free regularly when we have a tricky compensation case on."

His name was Edward Marshall Hall, who trained in his early years as an actor on the London stage, but decided to be a lawyer in later life and always said that his acting experience stood him in good stead in the courts. Father said that he rarely lost a case, and loved to come to Yorkshire. He would stay at the Queen's Hotel in Barnsley, coming to get the facts of the case at our house on Sunday morning and loving his breakfast of stew meat, which my Mum had been cooking in a big brown pot all night.

But to get back to my interview with Mr Douthwaite; When I'd finished telling him what I could about my Dad's working life, as it looked to me, he said that I'd done a very good job for him. But as I got up to go he told me again that it had to be a secret between us, just in case nothing came of it. From that though he must have made a good case out for my father, as a month later Dad got a letter from Buckingham Palace to say that he'd been selected to go on the Honours List.

A week later we were staying at the Adelphi Hotel in London as, when he'd got to know of my part in the conspiracy, he'd decided to take me with him to witness his Award. Joseph Arthur Hall drove us down, saying to me on the journey that it was about time someone gave my father some recognition for all his sterling work he had devoted to his fellow man. I agreed with him wholeheartedly, especially when he didn't say that I would never be as good as he was.

Joseph Arthur stayed with us at the hotel and once we had unpacked, took us on a tour of London town. It really opened my eyes I felt, as it was the first time that I'd ever been there. What fascinated me more than anything else was the British Museum where the men left me to look around, telling me to be at the entrance in an hour's time. I really needed a week to see everything that was there to see, but what fascinated me more than anything else was the Egyptian Room where time stood still, but also flew until it was time to go to the entrance to meet Dad and Joe. They'd been to 'wet their whistles' they said, and then Joseph said he'd take us to the Green Cockatoo. This was a restaurant not far from our hotel where they served 'Yorkshire Men's' food!

It was still war time though and food was rationed back at home to the last streak of bacon. However the restaurant must have had a special dispensation in our honour, I thought, because I had never had as much food which tasted so well in my life! 'Would these wonders never cease?' I thought to myself. But they didn't as we went back to our hotel to get ready for a show that was being given for the people who were on the Honours List at the Adelphi Theatre. And they were the best seats in the house! It was marvellous with really talented people on stage and took you completely out of your humdrum life into a happier one. Even my Dad laughed.

Joseph Arthur took us around London after breakfast the next morning on another bout of sight seeing, which I couldn't get enough of. I thought however that Father had seen it all before and was going through the motions for me. Then, at last, it was time for us to go to the Adelphi Theatre again to see my Dad on show. I sat with Joe Hall in the front seats and nobody was prouder than I when he was given his medal. The Minister for Fuel and Power awarded him with it, I can remember his words even now;

"Thomas Bird, I award you with the British Empire Medal for the unceasing work which you have done, and are still doing, for the mining industry. And, for which we give you our fervent thanks."

Then to my ears it sounded as though the theatre had erupted. But of course it could just have been my wishful thinking. To round things off we had a marvellous meal in even more marvellous surroundings before it was time to go back to the hotel and to get ready to go home in the morning.

It was one part of my life that I'll always remember, but for the life of me I couldn't tell you where his medal went. Probably to one of his grandchildren I think. Life though, after that little holiday, did seem to be aimless. So, our Leslie decided that it was time to introduce me to the Ship Inn, which was at the bottom of Ship Croft in Wombwell, to spice up my life a little. I'd already tried drinking beer, (although under age,) in the kitchen of the Little George in George Street where all the young drinkers started. Going in through the back door with my bosom friends I felt as hard as nails. However I can't say truthfully that I liked the taste of 'Slape Ale', as my Mother called it. I never told anyone however as I thought the acquired taste would come with time. Leslie took me with his pals and it was great to sit with them in a group when they'd had a few beers. The singers started to give voice and when they sang in harmony they sounded great. Well, at least to my ears they did, but it could have been the beer I suppose.

I also remember well that night feeling the bed spinning round once we were home. Luckily the bathroom wasn't far away for me to go and be sick. But the noise I'd made brought Leslie to my side, to hold my hand so to speak. It also woke Hilda, and it wasn't long before she'd worked out what had happened. She tried to clout my ear to impress onto me the error of my ways. It must have been a funny old sight that scene in our bathroom, apart from the pain in my sore ear. But it did stop me from going out with my elders, if nothing else.

19. Mountaineering

The war finally came to its end, with lives altered beyond all comprehension in some cases. Gwen went to live in Liverpool, where her husband John was the headmaster at a school in one of the poorer districts. He was determined to give his pupils some enjoyment out of life whenever he could, so every summer he took about twenty of them walking in North Wales. He was helped by some of his teaching staff, his friends and also me, in my official role as brother-in-law.

We stayed in youth hostels each time and on the first occasion we followed the coast, looking at castles which were very interesting. The boys enjoyed every step of the way. Some of them had never been on holiday in their lives before, and I can always remember getting to know them all, fighting in a heap on the carriage floor as it pulled out of Lime Street station to start our holidays!

When we'd all sorted our dialects out and everybody had given names to themselves we got on famously. Months before each trip John Tupman (Gwen's husband) would work out our route and would then contact the youth hostels to tell them what dates we would be arriving and departing. We usually walked an average of ten to fifteen miles between each hostel, depending on the weather of course, which in Wales we found out tended to be rather wet. But we cared little about that. Many was the time we found ourselves drenched to the skin but we walked ourselves bone dry and laughed as our feet tended to slosh about in our boots as we walked.

Usually there was a warden in charge at each hostel who greeted us when we arrived and helped us to settle in. Then they would put a meal on for us and very good they were too. Just to keep us in training we were all given jobs to help in running everything and when they were done our time was ours to do anything we wanted to do, but mainly we just rested up. We slept in dormitories which usually had comfortable beds. Even if they weren't though it wasn't long before we were in the land of dreams. Some of our sleeping quarters had been unusual things. I remember we once slept in a disused Chapel. Some of the pews had been left in position and as the lighting was sparse it was rather eerie, in the middle of the night it got more so.

We were all awakened by a hollow moaning and were terrified by the sight of a ghostly white face moving just on top of one of the pews. Howls of terror pierced the night and the more frightened ran to the other side of the Chapel. The braver ones, fascinated by the sight, decided to find how it was done. They soon found out that the culprit was one of our own of course. Aided and abetted by John Tupman, who'd lent him the torch to shine under his chin. Everybody got brave in an instant, laughing at themselves and telling him how well he'd acted 'the ghost'.

Sometimes we really had to forage like an invading army when we had no kitchen at the hostel to feed us. We ended up outside a rural fish and chip shop in one village, tired and hungry. We thought of filling our stomachs before walking on to the hostel, which was an old converted school. We queued for ages before a woman came to the door to tell us that they'd sold out. It appeared that all the villagers had discreetly been served at the back door of the establishment. 'Ah well it takes all sorts,' I thought secretly.

But we were not discouraged and sent one of the lads without his rucksack, (we'd learnt by our mistake,) into the local shop, where he utterly cleaned them out of tinned meat and vegetables. From there we went to the nearest farm to inquire from the farmer man if he could sell us some milk and potatoes. We waited with bated breath.

He sold us a half a churn of milk and said he wasn't sure about the spuds, but told us to look in the barn. When we did we found a little girl at the side of a heap of small blue *Pig Potatoes* who told us we could have as many as we wanted for half a crown in 'Pigeon English'. So we emptied our largest rucksack and filled it, not caring whether the pigs went hungry or not, with the unusually coloured potatoes. When we got into the disused schoolhouse, after we'd obeyed a notice on the door telling us where to go to find the key, there we found a kitchen of sorts, with all the utensils needed to feed an army, plus a dining room. The only drawback seemed to be the means of cooking the food, but low and behold, in one of the highest cupboards we found six fully fuelled primus stoves. And then everyone seemed to help to prepare our evening meal. I suppose it could have been because we were so hungry and that we'd prepared it ourselves, but everybody said after we'd eaten that it was the best meal they'd ever had in their lives.

As a surprise John once booked us in at a hostel against the mountain range of Snowdonia so we cold enjoy a bit of mountain climbing. He told us as we walked to the mountain range that there were different tracks or paths to the summit of the highest one, which was called Snowdon. The one we were going to climb was the one called the 'Pyg Track'. This was used by beginners, and from the bottom it wound its way around the mountain, which was graced by a hotel at the top. All the boys wanted to go and so did I, but the rest of the party decided to have a walk somewhere else. So, John detailed a young man, who I'll call E.F. who had been with him on trips before to lead us. When we left the hostel after our stay we were each given a packed lunch to sustain us until we reached our next port of call. We carried them in our largest rucksack and decided to have ours at the hotel at the top. We took them up with us as John had said that it was only a stroll, so off we went, this intrepid band of mountaineers ready for anything, and it's a good job we were!

Our path was marked by little piles of stones so we couldn't lose our way. Now whether John had engineered the position that we later found ourselves I never found out, but I can't think that he did. Our path gradually became steeper and the ground became loose stones, but that didn't worry us. What did was when we found out that E.F., who I'd noticed was gradually edging back from the front, had totally disappeared. It was just as though he'd turned himself into one of the piles of stones which we also found out had gone missing.

After having a brief conference we decided that we'd come to climb the mountain and so that's what we were going to do. Having decided which direction to go by a majority decision, which was upwards, we sallied forth. Looking back now however it was the wrong choice. We now found that the air was moving from cold to chilly and that the path had disappeared from view. We were at one with the mountain because it seemed to be at our side now and looking very jagged too.

I assumed command now, mainly because I was the biggest, and also because I was carrying the rucksack with all of our lunches in it. We stuck doggedly to our task with not a look back down the mountainside. Mist started to wreath around us and we heard the Rack and Pinion Engine puffing its way up the track. I'm sure most of us wished we were in the carriages which it pulled up to the summit hotel but if they did nobody mentioned it.

The going got really rough now and if we weren't straddling a sharp peak, with what seemed to be a bottomless drop on both sides, then I was taking my rucksack off to get it on its side through pillars of rocks, which seemed to be doing their damndest to stop us going any further. What made it more frightening was when the mist came down as we were on the pinnacles as if just to try to catch us out, but when it did we stopped climbing until it wreathed away. I learned later that the name of this so-called track was called 'Crib Gogh' which, when translated means 'Red Ridge'. What the red part of it had referred to I don't know because as far as I can remember the colour of the rock that we scaled that day was grey.

Nobody seemed to have a lot to say when we were climbing but I'm sure a lot of us were saying our prayers. After another half an hour, just when the upward climb seemed to be getting steeper, they were answered. The sound of the engine seemed to be nearer and the mist disappeared to show that we'd reached level ground. After walking along it for a while we came to something that everybody had been wanting to see; melting snow from the mountain top had made a stream that when we drank from, cupping our hands as makeshift beakers. It tasted like nothing we had sampled in our lives before. We rested there, slaking our thirst until our stomachs sloshed when we moved, before setting off on our trek once more.

Soon there before our eyes we saw the hotel, complete with train awaiting us. The next thing we did was to put down our stones, which we had been told had to be carried from the top of the Cairn the first time you climbed Snowdon. Then we made our way to the hotel where we intended to eat our sandwiches with a mug of tea.

Well, we were until we saw the notices on the walls of the dining room which stated that only food purchased from the hotel could be consumed on the premises. On our way outside we asked each other if we'd ever find this 'Welcome' that the song said that was in the Hillside and the Dale. We were all in one mind though regarding the way down, we weren't going back the same way that we'd come up! Down we went back to our spring-of-life where we ate our sandwiches and decided that, the quickest and safest way to reach civilisation would be to slide down the mountainside. We were all equipped with an army gas cape so we put them on and then looked around to find the slope with the least amount of boulders to bar our way. Then, after we'd all agreed on one, we sat on our bottoms and slid down on the grass, where we could find it. We walked when we couldn't.

The way was unclear at times and sometimes we had to double back on ourselves to be free of the massive rocks, but that didn't bother us at all. At times we could see, when we looked down, telegraph poles that looked like miniature matchsticks that grew in size as we descended. We were all happy with the knowledge that we were choosing the route we wanted to go. Then finally, we arrived at the bottom of the mountain with only the river Dee barring our way to the main road.

Without any waiting or debate as to what to do we walked through it, refreshing our feet marvellously on the way. Luckily as it was summer the river wasn't very deep and before we knew it, the road was under our feet, feeling very comfortable and safe. What's more, we all felt a sense of achievement, having beaten the mountain and then gotten down safely.

There was some debate however as to what we would say to E. F. when we saw him but, when we finally came to the rest of our party, (who were sitting under the veranda of the Mountaineers' Hotel, the 'Gorph Wysfa',) he wasn't to be seen anywhere. John Tupman must have decided that discretion was, in this case, definitely the best part of valour and had sent him on a hike. He did mention that they had been getting worried about us. We told them, not as worried as we were about us!

Then we gave them their crumpled sandwiches, which we'd taken up, and brought down Snowdon to eat. But to give him his due John said, "Not likely after your exploits! You can eat whatever they have on offer at this Inn." So we did, and a right royal feast it was.

Some of the youth hostels had been purpose-built for hikers and bikers and had showers built in them. I will always remember going for a shower on one occasion. As they were open I saw one of our group soaping himself down. I passed him but something different caught my eye and I had to look back, mystified by what I had seen. There, at the bottom of his back was a tail. It was about four inches long and was covered with short black hairs. I laughed out loud and thought how clever this youth had been to make something so realistic fixed it on to his bottom to withstand the flow of water as it did, and shot a hand out to pull it off. I nearly fainted when it refused to be pulled off and the lad turned round with a cheeky smile saying, "Go on have another pull. I wish I'd got as many pounds as I've had pulls on it!" I'm so glad that John Tupman saw it at the same time and could back me up when we talked about it whenever we got together with our relatives, who of course never believed us.

I asked the lad when he was dressed how he stopped his tail sticking out and his reply was, "The first thing I put in my pocket when I go out is a roll of adhesive tape." The next question I asked was "Does it ever embarrass you?" He replied "People who know me know what it is, and people who don't daren't ask." I thought how brave this youth was and then found I daren't ask him any more questions myself.

I still had to find out why E.F. left us in such a dangerous position on our first trip up the mountain so, at the first opportunity I had I questioned John. His reply was that E.F. liked to show off and lead people, who didn't know him, to think he knew more than he did. He said E.F. had told him that he knew the way that morning when he really didn't. I found this out the next day when we were leaving the hostel where we had spent the night. E. F. set off like a sprinter along the road, leaving everyone behind. John said quietly, "Everyone walk normally and we'll see what happens."

That's what we did, watching him speed along like an express train, but it wasn't long before we caught up with him and then passed him. He was entreating us from way behind to stop at the next farmhouse for some buttermilk. His pleas of course fell on deaf ears and we, the ridge walkers, felt a little satisfaction by his plight. We did however stop at the next farm who sold buttermilk to wait for him and all clapped when he finally arrived and all grudges were forgotten.

I went on these jaunts with John Tupman for a couple of years after the War and enjoyed them immensely, using all the tracks up to the summit of Snowden and most of the Hostels. But I never forgot the time when we were ill-led on the slopes and often wondered what happened to the boys who accompanied me. I'm sure they all did well as they were the salt of the earth.

Then it was back to work. I got a move from the little Blacksmiths' Shop on Silkstone pit hill and went back to the Shop in the pit yard, sharpening drills which the borers used to drill the coal. There were no more ponies for me to help manicure, but I never forgot Trixie and the gallops we shared from the field to the farmyard, which had been such happy days.

20. Changes

Then, when the weekends came round our gang of youths, who were all about the same age, started going around together. I think we were about thirteen in number. I remember it started with us all going on walks, that is after we'd been down to have a game of cricket or football depending on the season. We'd play on the Well Pitch in the Hilly Fields and then usually went to the Bowling Green cafe in Wombwell Park to have ice cream in lemonade, that is if we could afford it. Then, refreshed, we usually went walking, working the route out to end with our teatimes. Then as we grew older we started to go out drinking at night. We all met at the Horseshoe Hostelry which was in the middle of Wombwell's high street. From there we would go on a pub-crawl, calling at various pubs as we walked to the Drill Hall at Barnsley.

I never really liked to drink a lot of beer but as we all paid for a round in turn I had to get used to it. But I never liked it. A drop of lemonade would have made it a lot easier to drink but to think of the remarks ribald and otherwise that would have followed when I asked for a shandy, I didn't let the side down.

The Drill Hall was on Eastgate in Barnsley and was used by the Army during the War. Afterwards it was taken over by the Territorials. It was also used on Saturday as a dance hall for all and sundry, and when we used to arrive it was usually about an hour before the band played the last waltz. We were usually in no fit state for anything apart from rushing upstairs to the toilets to ease our bladders or to drop to sleep on a seat after being hypnotised by watching the dancers going round and round. Whatever we thought we were going to do inevitably ended with us doing the same thing as we usually did, walking home in a group, without a girl in sight.

But the discussion always was, as we wended our weary way home, how next weekend we wouldn't call at as many pubs, or how even we would catch a bus to show all the girls what we looked like when we were sober. So the next Saturday a majority decision decided that we'd just call at four pubs, two before we got to Stairfoot, (which was the halfway mark between Wombwell and Barnsley,) and two after.

But we never did get to Barnsley that night. After we'd left the Black Bull at Stairfoot we wended our way up the hill. We passed the Oaks Monument, dedicated to the men and boys who were killed in the explosion at the Colliery of the same name. As we came down the hill we heard the sound of music. We walked a bit further down and then found out where it was coming from. At the right hand side of the road was a church and on the gate outside was a notice saying that there, on this very night, a dance was to be held in the church hall.

'Manna from Heaven!' We hoped it would be full of girls, and us not even merry. I forget how much it cost to get in but it was well worth it as it was full of girls who we had never seen before. True, some came equipped with boyfriends, but that made it more of a challenge for a change as we had our wits about us.

It seemed we'd come to a Catholic church called St Joseph's in Kendray, a place on the way to Barnsley. We paid our entrance money and took our chances. I wasn't much of a dancer but in having a brief courtship with a girl who was a ballet dancer, I'd learnt to keep my feet from treading on hers too much, as she let me know in no uncertain terms when I did.

We were an unknown quantity to everybody in the hall when we came in. We sat on chairs with our backs against the wall to check on the talent when the band started playing. There seemed to be a shortage of male partners and a good numbers of girls were dancing with each other. I suppose really looking back, that they had checked us over with relish under lowered eyelids as soon as we came in. But I could be wrong! In those days you went to a girl who you wanted to dance with and asked her if you could have the pleasure of dancing with her. Usually they danced with you and while you danced, in your small talk, you found out as much about her as she was willing to tell you, and usually you told her as much about yourself as you thought she should know. And then you thanked her.

I think that it was an unwritten law that they danced with you even though they might not like the look of you. The first girl I danced with was sitting on her own and was looking as though as her next move would be to get her coat from the cloakroom and go home, but as I had been in that position many times I wasn't going to let that happen.

She smiled and said it would be a pleasure when I asked her to dance again, but was very clever at answering my questions with half-truths. Well at least that's what I thought, being a past master in doing that myself on the dance floor. I did find out later that she was teacher who worked at the local school but I left her thinking that she was a nice girl and would make a good friend but no more than that.

My dancing seemed to be getting better as I danced with most of the girls in the hall, but that could have been because my feet were going where I told them to for a change. Unlike most of the other times when they seemed to have a mind of their own, but I secretly thought it was John Smith's bitter that controlled them.

I had noticed a particular girl while dancing who stood out above all the others to my mind, so I kept her for the last. She'd been dancing with a tall young man who I thought must be her boyfriend, so I had misgivings about my venture. But once she was in my arms and I'd told her that my name was Frank Clarke and that my parish church was St Michael's at Wombwell, it was as though we'd been friends for years.

Will Shakespeare had got it dead right when he wrote "Oh what a tangled web we weave when first we practise to deceive," but somebody also said, (I just forgot who it was,) "All's fair in love and war." So I didn't worry a lot about a few white lies that I told her. It appeared that the boy she was dancing with was her brother and she also had another younger one with her. I danced with her for the rest of the evening finding that we danced well together and also were interested in each other. Her name was Patsy Galvin. At the end of the evening I asked if I could walk her home but she said that was what she'd brought her brothers for. She did however agree to meet me in the week to go to the pictures.

We met outside Boots chemists shop on Market Hill and went to see Al Johnson in *The Street Singer* at the Empire. She told me that she worked at the Share-Office at the Co-operative, while I explained my few white lies away. So began a courtship that had its ups and downs over the years, but was a lasting one. I spent a lot of time cycling from Barnsley back home during our courtship as the last bus was at ten-thirty and the time flashed by when we were together. So I started cycling there and could come back at my leisure. My steed was a BSA bike which had hung on the wall in the coalhouse ever since our Les had lost interest in cycling. He'd married a local girl so had no use for it. The bike frame, (for that's all that it was,) got all the necessary parts fitted in no time, and I also fitted a dynamo on the back wheel. All went well for a time, apart from when the rain came down and the back wheel didn't turn the dynamo. That's when I stayed overnight. My resting place was in a bed up in the attic at the top of the house, with a skylight window for ventilation and illumination.

Changes were on the way though. The Government, in their wisdom, decided that it would be better for all concerned if they gave the coal industry to the people. So, in 1947 on what was named Vesting Day they did, but kept all the officials in their positions. The only people who had to change jobs were the workers. Our Les went to work down the Pit while I got a transfer to Elsecar Central Workshops as it seemed that they wanted Blacksmiths there. Things changed on the Home Front too. I married Patsy Galvin in September 1949 in Holyrood Church at Barnsley.

Houses were in short supply for young couples when we decided to get married, but we had always agreed that we weren't going to live with either side of our families so we got lodgings. As it turned out a girl who worked in Pat's office had lodgings in Hemingfield and had been recently lucky enough to get a rented house. She told Pat that she'd see if she could get the landlord to consider us for her old rooms and luckily for us, he did.

21. Sheffield Wednesday

I will always remember going to Elsecar Workshops to be interviewed for my job. There were about five of us, all coming from different trades. We walked from Cortonwood along the Canal Bank. I suppose we were all filled with a feeling of foreboding, wondering what we'd let ourselves in for but never showing it to one another. In no time at we reached the end of the Canal, which stopped at the Workshops. We went past a Weigh, which was used for checking the loads of coal which were delivered from the wagon sidings nearby, and noticed on it's wall a notice. It said in large white letters on a blue background 'NO VACANCIES'. Were we on a Wild Goose Chase? But once we were through the gates a man came out of the Weigh and directed us to the Works Manager's Office.

He said, "You're in luck! Sheffield Wednesday won on Saturday!" The manager's name he told us was Leonard Lawson and if we were wise we'd call him 'Sir'. He also told us that Lawson had got the biggest pair of balls in Yorkshire. We found this out for ourselves when we walked up to his office. There, at our right hand side against the Blacksmiths' Shop, was a Fly Press. This consisted of long bar of iron with a cast iron ball at each end, which were indeed rather large. They operated a screw in it's housing and, when they were swung round, exerted a terrific bending pressure which I got to know about later.

I was so glad that we came in the daylight so that Mr Lawson wouldn't have had to be scrutinised by all of us in a peculiar manner. We were shepherded into his office by a young man who I supposed was his secretary. From there we saw a small man at the back of a desk which was, to my mind, far too big for him. He had white hair and a fiery complexion in colour and expression. I couldn't help wondering what he would have looked like if the Sheffield Wednesday football team had lost.

His manner though wasn't too bad at all. He gave us a tour of the Workshops, then told us as we walked round all the Shops which were well equipped, how they'd come into being. They'd been put together by the old Earl Fitzwilliam to repair everything that got damaged at his two Collieries which were New Stubbin and Elsecar Main. I had to marvel at the biggest lathe I'd ever seen which was in the Machine Shop. He said locomotive boilers were machined in it and they'd also got a lathe for machining wagon wheels in the aptly named

Wagon Shop. He also told us that he'd got to his position the hard way, by working in various engineering Shops in Sheffield.

To bring us to the end of our tour he showed us a block of stone built into the wall. It was above the outside door of the Machine Shop and chiselled into it were the words; *A Place for Everything and Everything in it's Place.* Mr Lawson pointed at it and said, "We like to keep things that way." Then he told us all to report to him the next Monday morning.

I'd noticed that everything that was able to be moved from its spot on my way round had 'E.F.W.' either painted or burned onto it. I thought to myself, "Shall we be tattooed to show everybody where we belong too?" So, I was already working at Elsecar Works when we came back from our honeymoon, which was spent in Somerset at her sister Josie's cottage. We had already moved our bits and pieces into our two rooms, (plus use of bathroom and toilet,) by courtesy of our Home Coal Leader. He also supplied us with a half ton of coal each month to heat ourselves as we had a fireplace. I'd already been down to the gas showrooms at Wombwell to get the longest gas pipe you've ever seen in your life, as the illumination was provided by gas, as was our cooking. This was to provide us with gas for our gas ring. I ran the pipe from the gas lamp, that had a turndown mantle on the wall in the corner of our bedroom, through the floor to couple up to the ring. This stood on a box in the corner of our dining-cum-sitting room. I sheeted the box with an iron plate on the top as a precaution against calling the fire service out!

We had a small three-piece suite and two chairs, plus a kitchen cabinet and all the accessories to sustain life, even if it was a bit cramped. However we had only ourselves to please. We lodged with Mr and Mrs Stenton who both worked at Cortonwood Colliery, he on the Screens and she nights in the canteen. Although we were living in the same house we each kept ourselves to ourselves. It was a semi-detached house which had been built by a local character called Billy Gedny, who had also built a bungalow at the side of it in which he lived. He could always be picked out in a crowd as he wore a hessian sack over his shoulders and, when asked why said it kept the cold out, but he was a very clever engineer. He used to go around all the scrap heaps in the area with his lorry and picked up things that ordinary people would have left. Then he fashioned them into yet another part of his travelling funfair. He also had a drift mine in his back garden from which, every Friday night, he pulled tubs full of coal with a haulage engine. These were emptied into a bunker which his lorry ran under to supply a cheaper type of fuel to local people. His enterprise came to a halt unfortunately when the seam of coal came too close to the local railway line.

To get to the Workshops from our lodgings I had to walk through three fields, passing in the last one the site of the gasworks which provided the illumination in the old days for the Works. The farmer who owned the fields always seemed to have livestock in one of them waiting for me each morning. The trouble was it didn't matter whether it was horses, cows or even geese. Whatever the breed, they all wanted to chase me. I always got through early, but safely. We started work at seven-thirty am, after clocking on at the time-office. Then I walked down to the Blacksmiths' Shop.

Just before the big double doored entrance was a large water pump with a cast iron tank in front of it. "No water piped into the Shop," I said to myself when I first arrived, "But it must get better?" Opening the door I saw a low roofed building with seven hearths against the farthest wall. There were two steam hammers, one in working condition and the other, a *Naysmyth*-style machine, was a museum piece. In the middle of the Shop stood a shearing and punching machine. This was not driven by a belt as was the one at Cortonwood, but had it's own electric motor operated by push buttons. Progress indeed.

Opposite me against the middle hearth was Bernard Baker the Foreman Blacksmith who I'd been introduced to on my tour. He also had a desk against the wall where he did his paperwork. I asked him about the old hammer and he took me up to it and said that the old Lord Fitzwilliam bought it and it was one of the first ever made by Alexander Naysmyth who had also designed it. In it's day it was the best ever made. It was situated between two of the hearths and could have been used manually or by a treadle. The other hammer, which was in use, had it's own air compressor built into it and was driven by electricity. But the method of operating it hadn't altered over the years from the old one.

Then Bernard took me up to the top of the Shop to show me the fan which supplied the blast for the fires. It made a booming noise when it was working in its house which adjoined the end of the Joinery Shop, pulling air from outside to push it through a channel in the floor to every fire in the Shop.

The workmen gradually came into the Shop and went to their respective workstations, reminding me of the time when I'd first started work so long ago. Bernard introduced me to his son Bill Baker, who was his charge-hand, with the instructions to show me where everything was kept. Then I was given a trade-test, making a double-ended spanner if I remember rightly. I must have passed the test as I was kept working there, helping to make everything that was required for the group of Collieries in our National Coal Board Area. I got to know quite a bit about the local area around there too. Some of it was rather amusing.

The present Earl Fitzwilliam had only one child, a son who was called Lord Milton. The family seat was called Wentworth Woodhouse as it was first constructed out of wood. However it had changed through the ages to the present stone built Wentworth House. When his son was born the Earl had a building made in Elsecar to commemorate his birth just opposite the Works, to be used as a community centre for the village of Elsecar. It was to be named the Milton Hall.

He also employed a local brewery to brew a special beer called *Audit Ale* which to be kept until the Lord got to be 21 years old. Then, to celebrate the occasion, a marquee was put up on the lawn in front of the house and filled with everything that anybody could wish to eat. While the brewery brought barrels and barrels of the highly intoxicating beer, everyone came from near and far came to help celebrate. They ate and drank with gusto until well into the night. The day after the fields on the way back to Elsecar from Wentworth were full of people looking for false teeth, trying many a pair for size after having lost the battle with a turbulent stomach. It was said that many husbands and wives shared a set of teeth until they could afford a new set each. You could say that the dentists had a 'Field Day' after the Lordie's Birthday!

Bernard Baker also told me that the male members of the Baker family had been Foreman Blacksmiths as far back as he could remember. His Granddad firstly, then his Dad, followed by his brother Marcus and then him. However his brother had not been a well man for some time. I remember Marcus coming to visit once and was surprised to see how big his rupture was. It just looked as though he was carrying another stomach. I always wondered why on earth didn't he have it operated on. I had my first one done in Barnsley Becket's Hospital when but a youth with no trouble at all, but I suppose he had his reasons for not doing.

The floor of the Shop was simply earth and just before finishing time, which was three-thirty pm. on weekdays, we had to rake it smooth and water it down ready for the morrow. Our working hours at the weekends were six am to eleven-thirty am, that is if we were lucky enough to get any overtime. Bernard was a workaholic and even when he was in between jobs he would be making washers at his hearth.

Bill Baker worked with a Striker making turns and crossings out of tub rails for all the Collieries in our area, just like Joe Smith did for Cortonwood. But where Joe worked to a drawing sketched by a Deputy on the back of a cigarette packet, Bill had a drawing to scale with all the measurements and radii on a blueprint drawn by the Collieries' own Draughtsman.

All the men who worked in the Shop either lived in Wentworth or Elsecar and I got on well with everybody, but of course I had my run-ins with Leonard Lawson in my turn. As luck would have it on one occasion, Sheffield Wednesday had just lost on the previous Saturday. I suppose he could always have had a puncture to one of his tyres on the Hercules sit-up and beg he rode to work on, (this was before he got his Austin Seven) to put him in such a bad mood too. But I knew he was spoiling for a fight the moment he came through the Shop doors. He walked up to where I was working, his eyes flashing like lightning and his cheeks with fiery spots on each cheekbone.

"What on earth have I done wrong?" I wondered to myself. There was nothing I knew off so I presumed he'd probably got me mixed up with some body else. Leonard, after watching me for a while, asked me what I was doing. Wanting to show him that I knew my stuff I went into a detailed explanation from the thread to the needle. However it wouldn't have mattered what I said, it had just apparently come around to my turn to be on the end of his wrath. After he'd told me that I couldn't tell him anything about engineering, and me asking him very politely why he'd asked me what I was doing then, he put me straight at the top of his hit-list. From then on he seemed to dog my footsteps wherever I was, but he never ever asked me again what I was doing. He still glared at me whenever he'd tracked me down though.

It wasn't long after that Bernard put me with his son Bill to learn how to make crossings. It was the time of the change over from tubs, tub rails, haulage ropes and ponies to mine cars, diesel locomotives and crossings, which were made from a stronger flat bottomed rail to take the heavier weight that the changeover caused. I got on well with Bill and his mate and was soon enjoying this new string to my bow. I did wonder why this had come about though, "Could it be that this was L.L.'s punishment? Me having to come out of the fire?" But it worried me not one jot, as long as they gave me my little tin on Friday afternoons with my wages in it, when I gave them my brass check at the pay office.

22. Smoked Out

All was well within my little world, which by now had gotten a little bigger. My wife and I by this time had become the proud parents of two boys and as a result of this in due time were offered, by the Wombwell Housing Committee, a 3-bedroomed semi-detached house. This was a newly built house not far from Bond Street where my Dad first lived when he came to Wombwell.

We grabbed it with both hands, even though we were smoked out of it when we lit our important first fire! I went to the Clerk of the Works to ask him if he could show me where the switch was to operate the fan which sucked the smoke out of the house when we thought we'd been kippered enough. He seemed to be a little annoyed at my remarks and said that this wasn't the time for levity, but I assured him that nobody in the house was laughing when it happened, more like coughing. It appeared that the bricklayer who had built our chimney, in his haste to finish the job, had dropped a couple of building bricks down the chimney. We had to live in the sitting room for a week until they'd knocked a hole in the chimney breast and had got their bricks back.

Then it was just a matter of putting every thing back as it was before, but when that was done and dusted, lo and behold large cracks appeared in our bedroom wall. So I just popped round again and brought it to their attention, saying that I understood why the housing list was so long; half of the bricklayers were employed in rectifying their earlier mistakes! It wasn't a remark which brought a twinkle into the Clerk of the Works eyes, but was one that I thought he ought to be told. This scuppered my plans however to ask him if he'd put a concrete path up the back garden where I planned to have a vegetable plot. There wasn't even a fence to separate our plot from next door's. But it certainly did have its advantages. We now had a sink of our own and so didn't have to get a bowl full of water from Mrs Stenton's bathroom to wash the children's nappies out in the front room anymore.

My wife was at this task one summer day with the front door open. She'd just got the nappies clean when she heard two dogs fighting outside our gate. In going to the door to see what all the noise was about she was asked by a man who was trying to stop the fight if she'd get some water to throw over the canines. Only too happy to oblige, and knowing where she could lay her hands on some, she got the water in the bowl and ran to the dogs. Unfortunately in her excitement she threw it high and missed the dogs. Much to the man's dismay she didn't miss him however as he was standing right behind them. His only complaint, as he spluttered through the dirty water, was that the temperature should have been cold. So to make amends she ran upstairs to the bathroom, filled the bowl with cold water and then ran downstairs to do exactly the same thing again! The dogs by this time had lost interest in each other and had wandered off. The man, who was an official from Elsecar Main I found out later, squelched off up the hill grumbling. I don't think he was well pleased and my wife was mortified. However when she told me about it I made fun of it and asked her if she'd requested whether it was cold enough when she'd thrown the second bowl?

Living in those rooms before our house had meant that Pat hadn't anywhere to dry her washing. Mrs S. wouldn't allow us to use her back-garden washing line so I decided to make a clothes horse to get the clothes dry in front of the fire. The only trouble about that was that I didn't have the necessary 'Wood-Note' which I could have had for a sixpence from the stores to allow me to take wood home from the Colliery. I was, of course, stopped with the pieces of wood slung across my bike crossbar as I was coming home from the night shift by the 'Hoyland Flying Squad'. They'd just been motorised and stopped me on the pretence that my rear light wasn't on. In the end the upshot was that the Colliery wouldn't press charges when they knew the facts. Tom Fowler, the Engine-Wright had me in his office to tell me that I should have gone to him and made my plight known. Then he would have had me one made in the Joinery Shop and he would have brought it in his car to my address, but the police weren't so lenient and I was fined five pounds and told not to do it again. From then on we had to take the washing to Pat's mother's at the weekend to get it washed and dried.

23. The Peggy Tub

The only trouble now was in order to get to work from Wombwell to Elsecar, I now had to catch a bus. It wasn't just a matter of walking over three fields, but we did have the advantage of having a fish shop at the bottom of the street. It wasn't very long however before I was getting a lift from a man who didn't live far away from us, who worked in the garage at the Works.

Bill Baker had taught me all the tricks of bending rails under the swinging balls and how to fit them together as required on the blueprints. He also became the Foreman Blacksmith when his Dad retired and left the rail job to me, complete with his Striker. I liked the job as it meant overtime and butter instead of margarine on our bread. It helped to pay our new furniture instalments to the Cooperative in

Barnsley too. But there were other jobs to do at Collieries in our area at weekends, as the people who lived in Denaby main village could tell you. We would go 'riveting' in the winding drum on nights. This was caused by something which had moved out of line, either in the bearings or in the drum shaft itself. This caused the rivets in the drum to loosen and the only time we could do the job was at night. So, every Saturday and Sunday night when the rivets had loosened we went to awaken the good people of Denaby. Normally this was just when they'd got off to sleep, but unfortunately for them they couldn't complain as we were making it possible for them to make a living. Everything went on smoothly at the Works until the overtime came to an end and for me, this meant having to find a new job.

I'd heard good reports of a steelworks at Stocksbridge called *Samuel Fox's* by men who'd left the coal industry, so I decided to give it a try there. I had a word with Bill Baker who said he'd be sorry to lose me but could well understand why I was going. He gave me a glowing testimonial to take with me. One Monday morning after catching two buses, I arrived at *Sammy Fox's* as it was known locally, in the rain. On the long journey I'd decided that Blacksmithing was really hard work so a new sort of job could be better, and a labourer's job for a start would be a good idea.

The first thing that we 'job-seekers' did was to see a film about how Fox's came into being. It showed how an umbrella manufacturer, unable to find a steel that was strong and bendable at the same time for his umbrella frames, decided to make what he wanted himself. So that was how Samuel Fox, "manufacturer of special steels" came into being. Then we were given a tour of the Works. This took quite a while, finding out that they made steels for everything from razor blades to ship propeller shafts. We had a meal in the canteen afterwards and then finally went for an interview to see what jobs were on offer. I was asked by a man behind a desk in an office, where compressed air drove message tubes everywhere at the same time it seemed, if I'd any references and what job did I last do. I told him and said that I'd like to be a labourer if it was possible. His answer was that they'd all the labourers they needed, but Blacksmiths were very sparse on the ground. In fact, he said "We want one just at this moment." I thought fate was against me but beggars can't be choosers so told him I'd accept the job.

His answer was, "We'll set you on to start next Monday when you can have your trade-test." I turned up then and was given a hearth in a well-equipped Blacksmiths' Shop. I was introduced to the Foreman Blacksmith who was aptly named John Smith, his charge-hand, (who was also his nephew,) and their secretary, who all worked together in what I thought was a very palatial office. My trade-test, John Smith told me, would be to make sure that I would be able to take my part in their very capable team of tradesmen. I was introduced to my Striker who said he came from Hoyland and was called Alan. Then I set about my task of making a pair of tongs, which was no trouble at all to me as they were to be made just as I wanted them, which made the job even easier!

There were two steam-hammers in the Shop, the one at the bottom was a ton one and the one halfway up a half ton one. Each had its own driver who sat at the controls. The hearth which I was using was at the side of the half ton one so I hadn't got far to go when forging, which made things even better. The previous Blacksmith, who had left to go to a better paid job, had also left a large box of tools. So I was well set up. Alan told me that he'd had a trade-test for this job and had failed to get it. But I decided not to inquire too closely about his failure as it must have been bad enough for him failing it. I thought to myself there must be some good working for Fox's as they employed people who were cripples, doing jobs that they could do. I had one such man driving the hammer for me. His name was Mick and he used crutches to swing from the toolbox, where we sat whilst waiting for the steel to get hot, to his seat behind the hammer. He couldn't use his legs at all but he was a marvellous hammer driver and the most cheerful person you could ever wish to meet. He told me that he regularly took part in the National Paraplegic Games and had won several medals at them. This I could believe as he could beat me to the hammer, even when giving me a head start any time he wanted.

Alan, my Striker, told me that his grandfather had been the farrier at Elsecar Main Colliery which was why he had got a job in the Blacksmiths' Shop there. He had come to Fox's like me, to seek his fortune. This was the best Shop I had ever worked in, not just because of its workmen and equipment, but also for the facilities that were provided. When we came in early in the morning we first went into the mess-room, where we put everything we wanted to into our own locker. Then went to the tea urn to make ourselves a pot to go with our breakfast sandwich as we caught the bus very early to get to work. There were also a row of toilets for us to use too.

The Charge-hand came round to everyone while we were still having a drink to give everybody a job. In my case on the first morning he told me what I'd be doing and so I got on with it. The first things I had to make were two pairs of tapered swages for the handles of the tongs. They seemed to be the only tools that were missing from the toolbox. You didn't borrow any hammer tools from other Blacksmiths as each had his own.

The only difference in this Shop compared with the others I'd worked in was the absence of a shearing and punching machine. Everything here was done under the hammers, but I soon got into the way of it. Things went well and I'd got one half of the tongs finished with the other just wanting the leg of the tong swaging. However I had to leave it at the side of the fire to go to the toilet. Unfortunately when I came back it seemed to have burnt into two pieces. When I asked about it Alan said he'd gone to talk to the Striker on the next hearth and so the draught must have come on its own. It was no use crying over spilt milk so I just welded the pieces together after showing Alan how to help with the job. They only did electric welding in the Shop and had no mild steel welding at all in the fire. Nobody said anything to me about it but think that they were surprised. No one ever told me that I'd passed my trade-test either. The Charge-hand just gave me another job when I'd finished the tongs.

When I got my first wage packet I was really glad that I'd moved to Fox's as being on shifts really gave me a good wage. The only drawback again was the travelling. I had to get to Hoyland to catch the bus to Fox's, after having walked up as steep hill from Elsecar first. I also lost a half hour when I finished my shift too because of the bus timetable. That wasn't bad when I was on dayshifts as I could call at the Victory Club for a pint, but I didn't have enough time on afternoons so I usually waited in the cold.

The Victory Club was part of the Work's social life where dances were held regularly but more so since the War, where the women hammer drivers used to work afternoons, wearing dance dresses under boiler suits. Then, after their shift they would 'trip the Light Fantastic' away at the Club. There was a Tool-Smith in the Shop who repaired and made all the lathe tools in the Works. He was the landlord of a public house in Stocksbridge called the Peggy Tub, where it was said his Striker was his best customer. He was always inviting me to go down for an evening, and I would have loved to if only to find out how it got its name, but I never had the time.

24. Rolling Mills

It was a long day with the bus journey thrown in. I enjoyed it though as it opened my eyes to the forging that was done there and the different tools that were used under the hammers. The other thing I liked was that the job that you were given at the beginning of the shift was the only one that you were given. Once it was finished you could make whatever tools you were short of.

When I was on afternoons and had got whatever we'd been given to do finished, I loved to go to the rolling mills and watch the huge ingots being lifted up from the soaking pits when they were white hot by great overhead cranes. Then they were moved over and lowered on to the rolling mills' conveyor, which led up to a great pair of steam-operated steel rollers. They were worked by a man in a glass windowed cabin which was directly above them. He opened the rollers up to take the ingot by its smallest end. These ingots had been cast in square tapered moulds in the Melting Shops for this purpose, so when the rollers pulled the ingot through it got squashed to whatever size was required. Then it was run back through them to be turned onto its other side by the same conveyor rollers to be made square by rolling through the mill again.

It was very steamy around the rollers as they were sprayed constantly by cold water to keep them cool, and it also removed scale from whatever was being rolled out. The operator worked to the instructions he'd been given at the beginning of his shift, rolling the steel out to the required dimensions. The final pass ran it along conveyor rollers that ran from the mill. The whole length of the rolling mill I was told, was equal to the length of the ship, *the Queen Mary*.

When we were shown the Melting Shop on our tour it seemed just as if we'd been welcomed into a 'Dante's Inferno' of heat, bright light and ear splitting noise, housed in a great cavernous building. Down one side of it were a row of electric arc furnaces, all in different modes of production. Some were being charged with an assortment of scrap iron, steel and all different metals. Whatever was being loaded, it was always accompanied by a series of violent bangs and cracks, together with flashes of 'lightening'. It was just like an internal thunderstorm. These furnaces were being filled through the use of overhead cranes. These ran from the stacks of material outside, which were attracted magnetically by a steel plate fixed to the cranes hook. When over the furnace, the crane driver lowered his load safely in before switching the magnetized plate off. Each knew from practice when he'd put enough material in and when he had, went to fill another one.

The next in-line could have been tapped and running white-hot steel into a huge ladle, to be taken where the ingot moulds waited in serried ranks. When full these would spit and shower sparks on its way. The steel was then poured into the bottom of the moulds, known in the trade as 'Upside Down Casting', which prevented impurities in the molten steel being included in the cast. All the furnaces and moulds had to be lined with materials to prevent the white-hot steel from burning into them, and teams of men were constantly working on this job.

25. Lock, Stock and Barrel

I was really enjoying working at Fox's, making the most money I'd ever earned in my life and getting to know things that I would never have gotten to know if I had stopped at Elsecar Central Workshop. My transport situation got better too as we moved to Barnsley and lived in a house on Caxton Street. Pat's mother lived on the same road and she helped us to put the down payment on the mortgage for it. Our first house that would really belong to us was a terraced one; Number 43. My wife was born in Number 33 and, like it's counterpart across the road it comprised a spacious attic, two bedrooms, a sitting room, kitchen and cellar. The cellar had a set pot for heating the water on washdays and a wall partitioned part with a door in it. This was known as the 'keeping cellar' which had a stone slab built up on bricks inside it. Food was kept on it to keep it cool. Next to this there was another wall with a door, behind which the coal was kept. It had a grate in its ceiling where from the road outside the coal could be delivered. And it was all ours, lock, stock and barrel.

As the trains ran just over the wall at the back of the house we really didn't need a clock as they were always on time. Funnily enough, the man who had lived in it previously was the gentleman who we'd bought our furniture from when we'd moved from Hemingfield to Rose Grove. He was called Mr Wilshee who was the Manager of the Cooperative Furnishing Department. Mr Wilshee had retired and moved to a bungalow once we'd bought the house from him.

When Pat and I first went to look around we went upstairs to view the house from the top. She whispered to me that Mr and Mrs Wilshee must have been frightened of the electricity going off, as the attic was full of small parafin lamps. Of course when I looked round I knew why they were there; The electricity supply only went as far as the bedrooms. The couple also collected pictures and had left a lot of them hanging on the attic walls. Some were quite good ones which stayed, but the lamps disappeared to be replaced by 100 watt bulbs.

Our clothes washing was easier for Pat too as her Mother was the proud owner of an electric washing machine and we had a clothes drier which lowered down from the ceiling by two pulleys and saved us a lot of trouble. The only drawback with these houses was that they didn't have hot water and the toilet was outside. In the kitchen on one side of the fire was a tank built into the fireplace. You could lift a lid and pour water into it, to be used when it got hot. On the other side was an oven with three shelves in it, closed by a latch on the door as big as used on any safe in the Bank of England. If you wanted a bath it was just a matter of filling the copper with water and lighting the fire underneath it. Then, when it was hot enough, you brought in the tin bath from outside where it hung on the wall. It was usually bath night for everyone on washdays. It wasn't long though before we had a gas heater fitted down in the cellar and one upstairs in the kitchen to make life a bit easier for all. We needed it too as our family was expanding.

26. Needhams

Unfortunately short time had come to Fox's however, just as it did to the Coal Board. It seemed that steel works were springing up in Europe and Japan which made steel cheaper than we could, so we lost orders. I worked it out and found that, with the bus fares and the cut in wages, it would be impossible for me to stop at Fox's, although I didn't like the idea of leaving the best job I'd ever had in my life. But life wouldn't be life if it didn't have its ups and downs, so once again I was looking for another job and for the life of me didn't know where to start.

Luckily someone who went to Holyrood Church, which we attended, got to know that I was after a job. He worked as a Draughtsman at *Needham Brothers and Browns* on Pontefract Road in Barnsley. They were in the market for a Blacksmith he told me and would I like to come and have a look around the Works to see what I thought about the job. On the sly he told me it would be mine if I applied. So I asked him how he could be sure about that, and he replied, "I do have a lot of say in who we employ as I'm part of the Managing Director's family. I married his daughter." "Fair enough," I thought, "Beggars can't be choosers and I do have to have another job. It won't hurt to have a look."

The next Monday morning I took a day off from Fox's and walked down Pontefract Road to see what was in store for me, thinking to myself, "Well if I don't like it, the world won't end and I could be bettering myself." On first appearances I wasn't very impressed. The entrance to the Engineering Works was through a small wooden door into a narrow passage which could hardly accommodate the clocking -in clock and the In and Out cards in their racks. But I thought again to myself, "It could get better." The man, who I took to be the Timekeeper, came out of his cubbyhole. Everything seemed to be on the small size that I'd come into contact with as yet. He asked me my business and I told him that I'd come to see the Foreman Blacksmith and gave him my name. He told me to wait and in a moment came back with him. He was a small, bespectacled and thickset man who took me on a tour around the Works, explaining that they were a closely linked family firm who made everything that a Colliery wanted.

We first went into the Blacksmiths' Shop which had three hearths surrounding a 5cwt compressed air powered hammer. To my dismay it seemed to be in the middle of a scrap heap. The compressor that drove it chugged away in a little house built inside the Shop and a profile burner fitted against the entrance with its operator in attendance. There was a big wooden door painted green which exited to Pontefract Road that I was told had to be kept closed unless there was a real emergency, for obvious reasons; truants were not tolerated. It brought back memories of waiting outside that door with my Mother when I was a small boy, because at one time the bus stop was there, and the door was open at the time. Looking back it must have been summertime and the workers would have been sweating bubbles as I saw them cutting the ends off great bars of material under the hammer when I looked into the Shop. One of the workers had brought the red-hot ends in a pair of tongs up to the door and I remember how the heat came from them and how I thought they were so brave to get so near to the heat.

Then he took me across the yard to the Foundry where the workers were in the process of casting a half of a Colliery-winding wheel. It must have been at least 20 inches in diameter when the two halves were machined and put together. The building was full of heat and fumes as the furnace, (which had been charged with a mixture of coke, limestone and pig iron which was then blown by a huge fan into molten metal,) had been tapped. The mould for the winding wheel half had been dropped below the floor level so that the molten metal could run down from the furnace into it. I noticed a man standing against the tapping hole with a lump of material in his hand, ready to stop proceedings if anything went wrong. As the mould was filled metal flames shot out at different places in it. My new mentor told me they were the gases which were being ignited by the white-hot metal and that they were a guide to where the metal had got into the half of the wheel.

From there we went into the Pattern Shop where a wooden shape had been made of everything that was to be cast, each in two halves. Each half also had an outer mould so that they were ready for clamping together and then filled with hot metal. When cold, the casting went to the Fettling Shop for the fettlers to take off the few bits of cast iron which had escaped from the mould, and then it was inspected. If passed the item in questions was then dispatched to whoever had ordered it.

I did tell the Foreman Blacksmith that the hammer didn't want material around it as it was, but if the job was on offer I'd give it a try, and at the same time he said he could give me one. The wage wasn't anywhere near as good as at Fox's but we could get by on it, so I said that I would take it.

The next day when I went to work I put a week's notice in and the dice, as they say, was cast. When I told John Smith what my resolution was he said that he was sorry to see me go, but could understand my motivation and that if he had been in the same position then he would have done the same thing too.

There was one good thing about my new job - I had more time at home now as I was working in Barnsley. I felt a loss though when I walked out of Fox's for the last time. It was also strange going down to Pontefract Road from Caxton Street, and then going through the narrow passage to clock on for the first time at *Needhams,* as it was known locally. My first job was sharpening, hardening and repairing all the tools that Barnsley Council possessed, and also making a few brackets too. Needhams had the contract for this. They also manufactured Haulage and Winding Engines, chairs or Cages or whatever you wanted to call them, which could ride men or coal into the pit shafts. Washery work seemed to be a specialist job for them too.

The Foreman Blacksmith seemed actually to be the only Blacksmith there apart from two youths who were in the process of learning the trade. As time went on however I had to acknowledge that he was the best smith I had ever seen. He did have one drawback though, he worked as though he had a train to catch and it was just pulling out of the station. He never seemed to walk wherever he was going but instead half ran. He told me that he first started work on the screens at Barnsley Main. I could only think that he must have had a hard taskmaster over him when he started work. The only time he stopped working was when he talked about Barnsley Football Club. It appeared that they'd just had a Blacksmith leave the Firm to work at the

Paper Mill, which was in Barnsley at the bottom of Old Mill Lane, which was how I'd come to have a job. Our working hours were seven-thirty am start with ten minutes for a break at nine o'clock. Then there would be a thirty-minute break for dinner and we would finish at four-thirty. There were some perks to the job however as we had our tea supplied free.

But gone were the times of one job per day. As soon as you'd finished a project there was another one waiting for you. I soon came to realise that that this Firm wanted blood as well as sweat and very often I used to drop to sleep above my dinner plate, to awaken with a start with my nose just above meat, potatoes and vegetables. Sometimes if we had a rush job on we worked Saturday, six o'clock till twelve, but it had to be required urgently. Working Sunday however, was out of the question.

We had to learn to live to our new income, just like the tailor has to cut his suit to his cloth. My dear wife never complained though. She enjoyed living on the same street as her mother, while I kept in touch with my family by making periodical trips to Wombwell. My mother had a bad heart and I can remember visiting her in Barnsley Becket's hospital in 1960 with our Les where she was in a coma. It was to be the last time I was to see her alive. My wife's mother also died the same year. Pat had always told her mother that she would never go to her funeral because they were so close, and in the end she never did. The day the cortege left Caxton Street she was in bed expecting our third child. We both listened to the clicks of the funeral car doors before they started on their sad trip. She had Stella, the first of our two daughters on that same day.

27. The Cutter Shop

I never did settle down at Needhams, possibly because the job before it had been too good to be true, but mainly because of the wage. The Directors of the Firm must have known they didn't pay their workers very well as they gave everyone of their employees a Christmas hamper that year. I got so worried about my state of affairs that I started taking a day a week off in order to look for another job. My first attempt was at a Clay Pipe Works just outside Penistone, but when I found out how far I had to go to get there I decided not to apply.

The next week it was Barnsley Main's chance to get me. I took the following Monday off, caught the Wombwell bus and got off at the top of Kendary Hill where the Oakes Monument stood at the side of the road. The Barnsley Main shaft had been sunk not too far from the Oakes site and I thought about the people who had been killed as I walked down the pit lane. I considered that they might have taken this same path, not knowing that it would be their last time to walk it. I quickly put these thoughts to the back of my mind as I walked to the railway bridge that spanned the track. This ran down by the side of the Colliery which I had to climb over before finally getting in to the pit yard.

Finding the Blacksmiths' Shop wasn't very hard, but nobody seemed to be in it. When I finally found the Foreman I asked him about a job and he led me to a table on which were various forgings and brackets. He then stood behind the table, much like a stallholder in Barnsley market showing off his wares. Indeed that's what he did do in a roundabout way. "Do you know what this is for?" he asked, followed by, "How would you set about making it?" I answered him to the best of my ability and after a few of these question and answers I decided to take the bull-by-the-horns. I said, "The proof of the pudding is in the eating thereof and, to my mind, talk is the cheapest thing in the world. The only way you can find out whether I can do your work is to set me on and find out. You can easily dismiss me if I don't come up to your expectations." Then he showed his true hand saying, "I'm not in a position to set you on. There's talk even now as I speak of closing one of our seams down because of a geological fault." So I said, "Why on earth didn't you tell me that when I first asked for a job? We would both have saved time wouldn't we!" Then I turned on my heel and left him, retracing my steps, not well pleased.

It wasn't many months after that, that Barnsley Main closed. By now I was in a quandary as to what options were in my sights. It was too late for me to change my trade. So, after thinking about it a long time, I decided to do something that I at one time would never have ventured to do, that is retracing my steps. I decided to test Bill Baker's promise. It was two years since he had made it and things could change in less time than that, but I was desperate. When he had last spoken to me at Elsecar Central Workshops, after giving me a glowing testimonial, his words had been, "If things don't work out to your expectations Frank you can always come back to us. Then, if I'm still at Elsecar, your job will still be here for you at any time." So I decided to visit the Works the next Saturday morning, hoping against hope that Bill Baker might be working.

The Sheffield train ran through Barnsley from Leeds and stopped at Elsecar so it was the quickest way of getting there. I wondered during the trip, as I covered familiar ground, what my reception would be. That would be if anyone was working at all there, considering that perhaps I was wasting my time. But fortune favoured the brave that day as the Time-Office was open and, when I asked the Timekeeper if Bill Baker was working he said, "Yes. Do you want to see him? He's in his Shop. I'll phone him and tell him you're coming to visit him."

It was strange going back into the Shop. The only thing that was different seemed to be the position of his office, although nothing else seemed to have changed. He welcomed me with open arms and said he often wondered how things had turned out for me. He also said that I was lucky to catch him working, the reason being that the painters were coming in to paint the Shop walls. So he'd got everybody in who wanted to work cleaning the roof timbers and walls in preparation for them. All the faces I knew were there, plus a few new ones, but everybody seemed to be glad to see me again. Bill took me down to his office and said "I heard things weren't going too well at Fox's. So it's true then." I told him everything that had happened since I left the Workshops. He listened intently, then said how sorry he was to hear how things had gone so wrong and realised why I'd come on a visit.

Unfortunately he hadn't got any Blacksmithing jobs going in the Shop at the moment. I got to my feet and was ready to thank him for giving me a hearing and to say 'Cheerio', when he stopped me and said, "Just a minute! I said there wasn't a job in **this** Shop. But I do know of a job that's waiting to be filled in the Cutter Shop, which carries the same wage rate as a Blacksmith's. I'll make arrangements for you to see the Cutter Shop Foreman on Monday afternoon at three o'clock. His name is Horace Saville and I'm sure that you'll get the job."

He was as good as his word and I got the job, which was repairing cutter machine jibs. These were used to cut out a gap at the bottom of the coal seam. Then the shot firers blew the coal down to be shovelled on to the conveyor belt by the Colliers, which in turn by a series of belts, ended up at the gear head. This was at the end of the conveyor belt which was raised up so that it could fill mine cars. These could carry a load of more than a ton of coal and could be pulled by diesel locomotives in a train to the pit bottom. It was the time of change in the coal industry and cheaper methods such as these were now being used compared to the ones used in my initial time in the mining trade.

So it was with mixed feelings I once more clocked on at Elsecar Workshops a week after putting my notice in at Needhams. I think everybody there who saw me had a handshake on offer to welcome someone who had strayed from the fold back into it. But after leaving the Time-Office I had to go in a different direction to which I was used to going to get to my new place of work and to meet my new workmates. I replaced the man who'd moved on from repairing cutter jibs, (which fitted into the machines,) to repairing the actual machines. Funnily enough the man who was to help me with the job I knew from my Cortonwood days. He used to work on the Screens there but I found out that he was doing the wrong job as he should have been a cartoonist. He could sketch people in no time at all and, with a pair of scissors and a piece of cardboard, cut a person's profile out like lightening. I was always telling him to show his skills to someone in the newspaper business but he said he only did it for fun which was a wasted talent to my mind.

I knew all about repairing cutter jibs as it was part of my job when working at Cortonwood. The only drawback was not having a steam hammer to forge under. It was a good thing that my Striker was a fitness fanatic and loved nothing better than forging a pair of tongs out on the anvil. Using his striking hammer instead of a steam hammer he said, kept him fit. We had a lot in common as he lived in Wombwell and knew people that I used to know. He'd started his working life at Taylor's Printers. They had a factory at the bottom of Station Lane and he'd enjoyed working there until *short time* had reared its ugly head yet again, and sent him on to pastures new. There were changes afoot not long after I'd started in the Cutter Shop too. More room was wanted to repair the cutting machines so we had to move up to my old workplace, the Blacksmiths' Shop.

We moved into a Hearth at the top of the Shop opposite the drilling machine. Times had changed as we no longer had to endure the 'Boom Boom' of the old fan which used to be up there, as now every fire had its own fan, which made it a lot quieter. We also had the advantage of being able to straighten the jib plates under the hammer instead of using our homemade press, made out of Dowry Prop cylinders in the Cutter Shop. I soon got back into the routine of travelling backwards and forwards on the train and there was the added asset of having Home Coal delivered to keep the home fires burning.

28. Rewards

I kept in touch with my Dad and two sisters, going periodically to visit them in Wombwell. Dad had started ailing and was always telling me when I was cutting his nails and trimming his hair that there was no joy in getting old. My elder sister, Hilda was still at home looking after him and my other sister Lilian had moved up from simply working in the Post Office to being in charge of it.

Things went on well at Elsecar and I settled back in to my old place of work without a lot of trouble, happy to be back. At the back of my mind there was always a niggling though. Fiery Len Lawson would have a down on me, as he was still the manager there, although I still wasn't sure why he had it in the first place. The only reason I could come up with was that he'd got to know about someone saying something about 'his swinging balls', and had got the wrong end of the tale, making me the villain of the piece. Just when I'd put the worry to the back of my mind however Horace Saville, my Foreman came to me to ask what I'd been up to, jokingly I thought. "Nothing that I know of," I said, "Why?" "Mr Lawson has just phoned up. He'd like a word with you. He could be wanting some fire irons making," he suggested with a smile. My thoughts as I walked up to his office were not on fire irons but that I had jumped out of the frying pan into the fire with my move back, and desperately tried to recall how well Sheffield Wednesday had over the weekend.

But I needn't have worried. His secretary ushered me into his presence and I couldn't help but think when I saw him that he'd never altered in looks. More to the point he had actually altered in his ways. He came from behind his big desk with a smile and an outstretched hand, saying how good it was to see me back and would I sit down and tell me how I'd got on with my previous employments. When I had done he said, "Everybody should move about in industry to get to know the tricks of their trade." and "It takes guts to move Frank. " He also said "I can't remember the times I moved about Sheffield learning my trade, but I know it gave me a knowledge that I would never have had staying in one place." I was tempted to look behind me to see whether there was someone else in the office he was speaking to, but didn't as I knew there wasn't. All I could think was that Sheffield Wednesday must have beaten another team at least 6-0, or that he was losing his mind, or nearer to the truth, he wanted something.

Then he said, "I'm in a bit of a quandary Frank and would like to know if you would help me out of it. Things have changed while you've been away. We've had a lot of orders for diesel crossings from many Collieries. Coal is now brought straight from the shearing machines at the coal face by conveyor belt to be loaded into mine cars which, as you know, run on diesel rails. Unfortunately we are behind with these orders and I wondered if you could help me out? I would be very grateful if you could." What could I say? So I said the only thing I could. "What about the cutter jibs? Who will repair them? I'm quite willing to help you out but what about Horace Saville?" He replied, "I've already had words with him and he says your Striker is capable of doing the job and we'll give him the rate for it if he'll do it." That was what I thought too and was prepared to take my leave, after asking him when I should start making crossings, to which he replied "Tomorrow."

Then he said, "I'm going to ask you another favour. We've got a Farrier on our books who's run out of ponies to shoe with all the changes. Could you show him how to make crossings?" It was no bother to me. The only trouble I could see was where we would lay them out. That was the first thing I asked Bill Baker the next day when he said it was great to have me back. There were plans to build a Crossing Shop at the side of the Blacksmiths' Shop he said but, for the time being, we would have to use part of the Plating Shop and also a stretch of the Fitting Shop, as well as outside the Blacksmiths'. It was a case of all-hands-to-the-pump at this time he mentioned, which was amusing as the big hand pump, which had been against the Shop door had just been removed to make way for the Crossing Shop. The swinging balls were also due to be removed in the near future.

Bill said that we could have as much overtime as we wanted during that time. He informed me that a rail and girder press had been ordered to bend the crossing rails with and that Hoppy Green, a local scrap merchant, had put in an offer for the balls but was refused. They, as well as the Naysmyth steam hammer, were destined to be moved along with the pump to a museum as part of English Industrial Heritage. It was another end of an era.

I'd never worked under the Naysmyth Hammer but had swung the balls about a bit and used the pump, which used water from one of the wells that dotted the Yard. The local people had always called the Workshops 'The Yard' before the Coal Board took it over, as they had never known it as anything else. It had first started its life as a rolling mill, owned by Earl Fitzwilliam and was used to make railway lines. After that it had developed into a foundry, casting iron and steel for industry. One of its entrances down Forge Lane was framed by a huge cast iron doorway which was probably made there. When I saw it for the first time it had been embedded into the wall although it belonged to an earlier period of the Yard's life. Amongst the other antiquities was a pumping engine, made by a Cornish engineer called Newcomen. It was installed by the Earl to keep the levels of mine water flooding his Collieries down.

There was a story that Henry Ford, the American magnate wanted it so much when he saw it that he offered the Earl a blank cheque for it but was refused. Then the Esso Petrol Company wanted to film it in action and they were given permission, provided that they footed the bill. The pump, which was a beam engine and a predecessor of the steam engine which Stephenson invented, only needed a capful of steam to work it. It pulled up water in leather buckets on its upstroke from the mine and emptied them into a trough on the down stroke which then ran into the Dove and Dearne River.

I remember well the two-inch wide steam pipe which was run from the boilers at Elsecar Main to make it work, and then seeing Arthur Chapman (who repaired steam locos at the Works,) starting it up for the moviemakers. Afterwards I watched it all on television again when it was screened. The pump, to my knowledge, is still at Elsecar in the position it was erected. However I don't think anyone has run it since that last time.

Everything worked out well for me. I got a new Striker and my old mate got a raise in wages, although he told me he didn't like the responsibility of the job. We Crossing Makers grabbed every bit of spare ground that was available to lay a turn on, especially if it had a roof over it. A local building firm started erecting a building to be the Crossing Shop alongside the Blacksmiths' Shop. The ex-Farrier came to work on the rails with us and also did a bit of charge handing for Bill Baker. Soon he was making crossings himself.

To my mind all things in the garden were rosy until, one day out of the blue, I got a summons from Fiery Leonard. Everything bad that could possibly have happened occurred to me as I walked up to his office. The message was that he'd like a word with me but my worry was, what about? I remembered the last time we'd met. That time we hadn't parted on fighting terms but instead had been very friendly. "Let's hope we'll be the same now," I thought. From that moment I decided, "Why worry about things that you don't know about? You've enough on worrying about things that you do." And so the only time I worry now is when there's a need to, much to my wife's annoyance!

Fortunately I found out when he greeted me, that things hadn't changed between us. In fact he seemed to be more friendly than before, thanking me for helping the Farrier to add another string to his bow. Then he asked what could he do to help me as I'd helped him? I said it was part of the job to show others how to do things as I'd been shown and I was only too glad to do it. Especially since I was re-employed here when I wanted a job again, but he wouldn't hear of it and I could see his bottom lip starting to jut out which was a sign of him beginning to get angry. "Anything for a quiet life," I thought so I racked my brains. What did I want? Then I remembered. What I wanted more than anything else was a wooden bench for the cellar at home. We had a bare wall there that just cried out for one, but I then remembered the trouble that had happened before when I'd gotten involved with wood-work.

So I decided to take the bull-by-the-horns and tell him of my fears. L.L. smiled at my words and said, "I was appointed by Earl Fitzwilliam to be the Manager of these Workshops and, to my mind, I do the job very well. If I didn't I wouldn't be doing it would I? And even though we're called the National Coal Board now, what I decide to do gets done. Whatever you want making draw it, complete with dimensions, and give it to the Foreman Joiner. I'll have a word with him and rest assured, it will be delivered by the Work's lorry to your house." So, crossing my fingers, I measured up down in the cellar and completed my instructions. It seemed in no time at all that I was the proud owner of the best oak bench you could ever wish to see.

With three teams of men working on crossings and an abundance of overtime it wasn't long before we got the backlog out of the way and could work back on the run-of-the-mill jobs. One job I distinctly remember doing was putting two brackets round the chimney on top of the Newcomen Pump House and I often wonder if they are still up there.

Change was in the offing yet again however. Central Workshops throughout the Coal Board were going to be reorganised into repairing just one of the items which were required by Collieries to produce coal. In their wisdom, the High Command decreed that Elsecar Workshops would repair powered roof supports. The days of holding the roof of the coal seam up with wooden bars or planks, with pit props wedged underneath them while the coal was extracted, was long gone. Everything that could be was mechanised. Hydraulic props, driven by water pumps on the coalface, lifted cantilevers under the roof of the coal seam to take the weight. Another part of the support pushed the panzer chain. This carried the shearing machine on top of it up to the coalface using hydraulic props again.

There was also a change to automatic coal cutting. The shearing machine moved up the coalface on its anchored chain, digging its many-toothed shearing drum into the seam. This would send the coal on to a scraper chain which lay in the bottom of the panzer, to be delivered on to a conveyor belt.

So everything had to be organised with a view of working on the repair of powered supports at Elsecar Workshops. One of the first things that we had to do was to move out of the Blacksmiths' Shop. This was going to be done in stages. The Crossing Shop was to be used as the Leg Shop, where all the hydraulic legs were to be repaired. Our new place of work was to be in a building that had housed the old Wagon Shop which had a shot-blasting machine and an overhead travelling crane in it. But in the meanwhile we had to manage where we were working on the powered supports while we gradually transferred our hearths, drilling machine and hammer up to our new home.

The trainee Crossing Maker retired and I was asked if I would take his place as Charge-Hand and said yes as it meant I earned a bigger wage, but also carried more responsibility. Bill Baker was still the Blacksmith's Foreman but seemed to spend a lot of his time up in the Planning Office, ordering materials for various jobs that were in the pipeline.

29. How the Other Half Live

During this second period of time at Elsecar I was sent out to Collieries, usually at weekends, together with other men to help repair machinery that could only be stopped working then. It helped give me more experience. Then I worked quite a long time on nights at Cortonwood Colliery on what they called 'the bunker track' in the Silkstone Seam. Someone had had a great idea of filling steel wagons, which had open bottoms, with coal and which were coupled up in a train. Instead of bottoms the wagons were sealed with a rubber conveyor belt and were filled with coal on the dayshift. Then they were emptied into a huge bunker to be wound out of the pit on the nightshift. The firm who designed and made the haulage engine which pulled the wagons over the bunker was non-other than Needham Brothers and Brown. In another coincidence, the man who installed it was none other than my friend who had got me my job at the firm. He was surprised and pleased to see me there.

The wagons had been made at the Chesterfield wagon building company of *Butterley's*. They were delivered stripped down as far as they could be so that the shaft-men could sling them under the Cage on the nightshift at the Silkstone Shaft Low Landing. Then, after being lowered down the shaft, they were put onto timber trams and moved to the place where we built them on top of the conveyor belt. This was done very carefully as we didn't have a lot of room to spare to get out of the way if a wagon side happened to slip while being held in position by the lifting blocks.

We tried to assemble two wagons per shift. Sometimes we could and other times we failed miserably. When we'd built one we had our break for a sandwich and a drink. The roadway or 'heading' where the bunker track ran had been cut out of what looked like rock to me, but still had what they called 'rings' set underneath the roof at intervals. These were steel girders in sections fish-plated together with corrugated pieces of steel fitted between them. To my eye however it still seemed a poor protection against the millions of tons of material above our heads, but it seemed to do the job very well. The Deputy who came around to see if everything was okay with us during the night said that, when the weight came on as it did, it was when the strata moved. Then the floor, as well as the roof, altered. He said sometimes the roof came down and the floor bellied up, which was very enlightening in its own way. However it made our little band, when we had time, cast a cautious eye on the floor as well as the roof.

He added, (for he must have seen the look on our faces,) "The surveyors chose this place for the bunker road as the heading was cut through solid rock and will never move to my mind." He was a Deputy I remembered seeing down the pit when I first went down. I can recollect him teaching young boys, who had just started working in the pit bottom, to read during their snap-time with the aid of comics. Arthur, that was his name, had missed his vocation in life. He should have been a schoolmaster as he was never happier than when he was explaining something to people.

One particular snap-time he took us on a 'Voyage of Discovery', as he called it. "To see how the other half live!" he remarked. After a torturous route, sometimes on our stomachs and sometimes having to ride on conveyor belts, we followed him to the coalface. It must have taken us a half hour to get there, but once we were we realised it was well worth the trip. It was a hive of industry, lit by compressed air driven lamps casting an eerie blue glow over sweating Colliers. In the dusty environment they all worked together to one purpose, making the earth give up its coal. We didn't stay long as we knew we were in the way and so retraced our way back to what we thought was normality. Afterwards we set about our task with renewed vigour after seeing what the Colliers had to put up with.

To start our shift we had to clock on at the Workshops at nine-thirty pm before we were taken to Cortonwood by the Coal Board van, which was waiting for us. It was driven by the resident driver who lived with his wife in a house in the Workshops. We arrived in time to get changed in the Baths into our working clothes, then to get our checks from the Time Office and finally went into the Lamp Room to pick up cap lamps complete with battery. Then it was just a matter of walking up the steps to the pit hill where we gave the Banksman our checks which he put into the In box to show that we were down the pit.

Finally he searched us all for cigarettes and matches before we went in the Cage. He had to search us as some Colliers were so in love with Lady Nicotine that they weren't averse to smuggling her down the pit for a crafty suck and blow in the workings. However this could have a deadly outcome for us all. The only tobacco that they were allowed to take down was 'Thick Twist' which they chewed to ease the ache and forever spat the juice which they made out of their mouths.

The bunker road soon got finished and went into use. Luckily weren't asked to go back, so everything must have worked all right. Our main job now was moving everything we needed to the Wagon Shop. We weren't able to move all the hearths because we hadn't enough room there so we just used three of them. It was enough though as there wouldn't be as much forging as we did before. But we did take the hammer and installed it in the middle of the Shop. It was used to straighten parts of the supports which required repairing. In addition we also had a large shot-blasting machine at the entrance. This was used to clean the supports before they were fork lifted down to the Plating Shop to be repaired. Half of the Plating Shop had been used by Ernest Riley who repaired locomotive boilers for the area, before that is, that we were told of the decision to give us the powered supports, so he had to find a new home.

30. Crack Detection

It was about this time that I was told that I'd been enrolled at a College in West Bromwich to go on a course of *Non Destructive Crack Detection Inspection*. All the men who worked in the Cage Suspension Department, who checked the suspension gear, had been on this course and had to pass an examination to do it. It appeared that naturally, if I was going to sign the certificates in my newly promoted role, then I had to know what it entailed. So, after being told to put down all my expenses while on the trip, I set off one Monday to catch a train from Barnsley to get to Sheffield. Then onto West Bromwich via Birmingham where I was met by the 'Dame Margaret Hall Bus'. Together with a few more faintly bewildered gentlemen we were transported to the town of Washington. Dame Margaret Hall, when we got to it, was a boarding school where our group of about thirty men were to stay while commuting to a College of mechanical technology. Here we were to find out how cracks in metals came to be made and how to find them.

One of the first things we did find out however was that we ought to have brought a ball of string with us. Then we could have tied one end of it to our bedroom doors when we left in the morning and then paid it out until we got to the dining hall to tie it off there. The rooms and beds were quite comfortable though when we finally found them again after tea! We slept two to a room, in single beds of course. Unfortunately for me the other occupant of my room snored like a sty full of pigs. I took it in my stride though, used to being the recipient of 'Sod's Law'.

Rather than the schooling it was the layout of the place that taxed the brain. The corridors were low and not very wide, with no arrow or direction posted anywhere, (much like being down a pit). We decided it must be part of the learning trend that we were about to receive, but it was remarkable how quickly we found our way to the kitchen late at night when we were acquainted with the fact that a case or two of Newcastle Brown Ale had been laid on for our disposal there.

The other students at the hall must have been on holiday for a fortnight because that was the time during which we were to be taught the mysteries of 'crack detection'. I can remember the first morning that we were at our desks at the college, a mixed bunch of varying ages, wondering what on earth what was going to happen next. We soon found out though as our tutor gave out a sheet of printed paper to each and everyone of us. He told us to put them on our desks the blank side up and not to look at them until he said to.

When he did we found it contained a welcome to the College at the head followed by a list of the most stupid things to do with our nearest partner such as asking him his mother's maiden name and his father's date of birth. The second to last instruction told us to bang our desk lids down three times! But it was the last request that counted. It said at the bottom of the list, "Ignore the rest of these instructions, sit still and fold your arms." That gave us a clue to who had been there before - the ones who hadn't moved or spoken apart from folding their arms.

When we'd all finished the tutor said he wasn't going to apologise for making a lot of us look like fools. It had been done for a purpose, to make everyone of us remember the morning when you may make the mistake of acting on instructions before reading to the end of them. The mistakes made today could of course be rectified, but given other circumstances, especially in our line of work, impatience could have a fatal ending.

He then introduced himself and then said it was quite safe to introduce ourselves to each other now, which we did, smiling foolishly at one another. Our tutors consisted of a male and female who knew all there was to know about crack detection and who had worked in factories all over the world during the Second World War, training would-be inspectors. They really did know what they were talking about. The idea, they explained, was to find surface cracks in manganese steel, which all suspension gear was made of these days.

We were given a good grounding in preparation and examination of varied objects, some that we'd never seen in our life before. Others however, were part of our daily working lives. In the short time that we were there we made some good friends, as we usually worked in pairs and also went out together around the Working Men's Clubs at night. There seemed to be a Club in every street and each one had a dance floor in it, complete with a four-piece band in attendance. We had trouble at first getting used to the dialect, but we were soon able to make the barmen understand what we wanted to drink and we were welcomed with open arms when we explained where we came from and why. It was of course a mining community that we were visiting, not far from Ashington Colliery and the Central Workshops there. We must have tried at least six Clubs in the short time that we were there and enjoyed them all!

We also watched football, one Saturday West Brom and the next Saturday Aston Villa. Luckily while we were there it was Independence Day too so we watched the goings on of the ceremonies performed. As it was in Washington, where George Washington's ancestors had come from, we saw they still kept alive the knowledge that his roots were from that part of England. At the Town Hall the Stars and Stripes Flag was pulled to the top of the flagstaff to the accompaniment of kettledrums and bugles playing 'The Star Spangled Banner'. We'd been given time off from our studies to witness this historic event and went to visit a museum there where we saw uniforms and clothes that Washington himself had worn when he was alive, all displayed in glass cases.

The drums and bugles took me back through the years to my time in the Boys Brigade, which I'd really enjoyed until 'Corporal Punishment' had reared his ugly head. But in no time at all we were back at work at the College. Our working partners were changed several times and you could find yourself with anyone, including a Scottish Chief Inspector as your mate. He informed me that he'd just flown down to have a refresher course while another young man from the East Midlands told me he was just learning the ropes. We were given tests along the way, to make sure I suppose, that they weren't wasting their time and ours with their endeavours.

Finally we had our last one, which was rewarded with a certificate to prove to all and sundry that we'd made the grade. Then, after much hand shaking and telling each other we'd keep in touch, (which we never did in fact,) we were all back on our journey home.

The experience had been beneficial to my job, and meeting other people had been enjoyable. It was however good to be back home and to find that nothing earth shattering had occurred while I'd been away. The only thing that had changed concerned our Harold, who had married and gone to live in Hemingfield during the War. He had now left his job as a Park Keeper and had come to work at the Cotonwood Colliery in the Fitting Shop as a Fitter's Mate as the new job paid more.

31. Bird Watching

When I was younger I would often take Harold's Springer Spaniel, called Skippy, for walks in the Hilly Fields. It was a liver and white coloured dog who loved jumping above the long grass and found me countless bird's nests by landing near the unsuspecting bird on the nest and causing it to fly up in alarm. He also dropped in on many a courting couple, much to their annoyance. When he did I distanced myself as far as I could from him. But he did help me fill two tin boxes full of birds eggs, which I rested on beds of cotton wool after blowing them. At that time there were no laws against taking eggs from nests.

It was our Les of course who taught me all about bird nesting on the walks he used to take the younger members of the family on. These were usually on Sunday afternoons. We used to walk to all the local beauty spots and then get back for tea. One Sunday morning we set off on our walk very early. I think that my transport must have been a pram because we went to visit our Grandma and Granddad Clarke who lived at Grimethorpe. It was a long walk going up to Stormhill Woods and then through Brierley Common before we got to their house. When we got there Granddad was sitting on a stool in the middle of the red-bricked floor of the kitchen. He was peeling potatoes for dinner and pretended he didn't know us, saying that whatever we were selling they didn't want any, until Grandma came in and threatened to box his ears. Then he welcomed us with open arms, saying it was so long since he'd last seen us he'd forgotten what we looked like. We enjoyed our stay there and I think we must have stayed for a few days.

I can remember being in Grandma's bed looking at the coloured pictures in their family Bible. My Mother once told me that her Father, my Granddad, was a Deputy who worked at Grimethorpe Colliery. At one time when the Colliery was on short time he decided to try his hand at digging for gold. He and a few of his workmates boarded a ship and sailed to South Africa to make their fortunes. They worked in the gold fields near Johannesburg but didn't stay very long as they didn't find a lot of gold, but did find the heat and flies too oppressive for them. Another thing that put them off was catching the Native workmen they employed filling their drinking water bottles up with urine. My Mother said that when they returned home nearly every household in Grimethorpe had a Native-made Calabash bowl and a walking stick.

32. Promotion

Back at Elsecar Workshops, things were altering once more. Leonard Lawson had decided that he wanted to watch Sheffield Wednesday play away as well as at home and so retired. Being 'Rationalised' and turned over to work mainly on powered roof supports could have had a lot to do with it I thought, but a change is as good as a rest so they say. So we had a new manager to contend with, plus a Superintendent to help him rule the roost. To make their positions more secure a General Foreman was employed.

Bill Baker was still working between the Blacksmiths' Shop and the Planning Office while I did my stint as Acting Foreman, although being paid Charge-Hand's money. I decided that this couldn't go on and went to 'Beard The Lion in its Den', which was a saying of ours. Namely it meant that I went to see the Manager in his office. He told me that they would have to publicise the Foreman's job when Bill Baker actually got the job in the Planning Office, as that one would have to be advertised too. My reply was that they would have to get a move on with the advertising or they'd shortly have to advertise for a Charge-Hand for the Blacksmiths' Shop too.

That was my first conversation with our new Manager and we never saw eye to eye for the rest of our time together, but it did bring matters to a head. In no time at all it seemed, Bill Baker moved officially into the Planning Office, although I never did hear of that job being advertised. Then again, I probably didn't look closely enough.

The Foreman's job was advertised however and I put my name down for it, not caring really whether I got it or not. I expected grief from day one if I got the job after my head-to-head with the Manager. Funnily enough I was the only to apply. Then I got a message from the Manager telling me that I had been successful in my application. The letter also told me that from now on I would be placed on the *weekly paid industrial staff* and instead of clocking on, would be signing my name in the Time Book.

I was also informed that I would be paid the Foreman's rate and from that time would be superannuated. I was issued with three white smocks and a black duffle coat too, well 'we Foremen' had to have some sort of badge of office I suppose, and the workmen had to be warned when we were on the way. I had the help of two Charge-Hands who I picked from my workforce, one for the Blacksmiths' Shop and one for the Cage suspension gear department. However what I really wanted was help with the amount of jobs that suddenly appeared out of nowhere.

As well as running the Blacksmiths' Shop I had to keep an eye on the Cage Suspension Department where a lot of paperwork had to be checked, signed and sealed and then delivered with the help of the Manager's typist. All the suspension gear that we checked had to be certified to say whether it was safe to be used and, if it wasn't, the certificate would say it wanted replacing. Safety was paramount in the Coal Board. I had to check all the machines first thing every morning in the Shop before work started to see if they were in working order to a checklist which ended up in the Manager's office. The Shop's temperature had a space to be recorded in on the list too as, below a certain heat working wouldn't be allowed. Above a certain one wouldn't either.

After a few months getting used to the job there came a request from the Management. I was told that in order for the 'Powers That Be' to be able to get a hold of me in a hurry, they would like me to live in Elsecar. That put the cat amongst the pigeons as our family now had got larger and we had another boy and girl, Theresa and Stephen. We were also happily settled down in Caxton Street too. So it was with a heavy heart that I acquainted my wife with the fact that a move was in the pipeline, knowing all the upset that it would cause. But she took it in her stride, Barnsley not being the same place for her since her Mother had died. She said, "Let's look at the house they've given us to live in first though."

During the War coalminers were urgently needed, and so were the houses for them to live in. The Government had decided to build some quickly and they were called 'Prefabs' from the term 'prefabricated houses'. These were usually made from concrete slabs so that they could be assembled in a very short time. Quite a few of these were built in Elsecar for Scottish miners who had been redirected from Scotland by the Ministry of Fuel and Power to help with the War effort.

It was to two of these Prefabs that we were directed to view as a possible new home. They were located on a street called Welland Crescent. One had three bedrooms plus kitchen, dining room and sitting room, but the other one that we looked at had four bedrooms, so we decided on that one. There wasn't much of a garden to cultivate, just a bit at the side and back, but that suited me fine as I intended to buy a greenhouse and grow flowers. Opposite the side door was an outhouse and next to that a coalhouse.

The coal fire in the kitchen heated the house by radiators so we were warm and snug. The rent was taken out of my wage before I got it so it seemed to be free. The only trouble that we would have was which school the younger children would be able to go to. Eventually we got them places at a school in Hoyland called Saint Helen's. Unfortunately the town was a fair walk up a steep hill if you missed the bus. John and Anthony still went to their school, Saint Michael's at Athersly near Barnsley, and Stella only stayed a year at Saint Helen's before she moved to Notre Dame Girls' High School at Sheffield, travelling by train to get there.

We changed from shopping at Barnsley Market to Hoyland's local shops and got used to it in time. We still went to visit Pat's Dad and her sister, Mollie, who was a teacher. She taught in Barnsley and still lived with her Dad. He was called Thomas and, just like my Dad, was the Secretary of his Union which was the National Union of Railwaymen, L.N.E.R. Branch. I always thought that was very remarkable and will always remember him giving Pat and myself a ride on the footplate of the 'Push and Pull Loco' to Penistone and back. There wasn't a lot of room on the footplate as the Fireman had to keep stoking the fire up and we had to move out of his way when he decided it was time to throw a few shovels full of coal on. But it was thrilling to be speeding through the dark with the firebox glowing and the smoke billowing up through the smokestack. It ended all too quickly for me, but I didn't think Pat minded at all when we got back. She was glad that we'd walked up from Barnsley Court House Station in the dark where her Dad had dropped us off, as we could have gone on the Theatre Royal Stage in the midst of a troupe of Kentucky Minstrels without using grease paint. We didn't find that out however until we looked at each other in the light!

Pat told me that her Dad had been pulled over the coals many times for setting the woods on fire through which he went when he was on the Penistone Run. Every time he told the 'Powers That Be' when he was called to the office to give a reason for it, that in each case he'd been running late and as he was such a stickler about being on time, he'd had to put a bit more speed on. My father-in-law was a very talented and kindly man. He was a great artist and when I saw him for the first time he was working on an initial from the Book of Kells which he'd drawn from memory and was illustrating it. He was a quiet man who was at his happiest when at the seaside, using a child's spade to draw out enormous outlines of faces, animals and dragons. Then he would invite children who were on the beach to help him outline them. In no time at all he would be organising hundreds of them, who'd left their castles and moats, to take part in his 'Sand Paintings' as he called them, and they all asked him when he was coming again.

Theresa, our youngest daughter, was educated at Saint Helen's School after Holy Rood School at Barnsley. From there she went on to Pope Pius' School at Wath on Dearne as the Education Authorities in their wisdom at that time, had stopped the Eleven-Plus Selection. As she had always wanted to be a nurse, when she was sixteen she applied to the pre-nursing school at Barnsley District General Hospital for a place and got one. After two years I can remember going to the Arcadian Hall at Barnsley with Pat to see her certificate that entitled her to be a R.G.N. or a Registered General Nurse, which were presented by the Master Cutler of that time. She couldn't be there to receive herself because she had been living in at the hospital in the Nurses' Flats. That was until the Governors of the hospital decided to raise the rents of the flats by a good deal more than the small rise that they'd given the nurses.

She was working at Barnsley District Hospital when our Les was in hospital and diagnosed with inoperable cancer. He knew about his condition and when Theresa visited him, as she did at the end of her shift, he used to tell her of his worry about his family, whether they knew about his illness and would it be the best to talk about it with them. To the last he always thought about other people's feelings. Theresa was a girl of spirit and had a lot of her great Aunt Maria's blood running in her veins. Just like her, she couldn't stand been victimised. So, when she saw an advertisement asking for nurses to work in Germany she applied, even though she couldn't speak a word of German. She had the will to learn though. Firstly she went to work at an old people's home in Germany, learning how to speak the language until she was fluent enough to work in a hospital.

She progressed in leaps and bounds and eventually worked her way up to be an anathetheist in a team which would be called from the hospital she worked at. She told us when she came home on holiday, that they travelled sometimes in a Sea King helicopter to the islands around Germany when required. It was on one of these holidays that she met her husband to be. Nigel went to Germany and brought her home after proposing to her. After that she came back and went back to work at Barnsley District General. This time there was no trouble about the flat rents as she bought a house of her own to live in which was just a walk away from the hospital.

Our other daughter Stella went to University where she trained to become a teacher and John our eldest went to work in the offices of Barnsley Markets. Just like his Uncle Harold before him however, he didn't take to office work and decided to join the Royal Air Force. Anthony went to work as an apprentice welder for a local engineering firm while Stephen, our youngest son, went to Pope Pius School and then to a school which had a sixth form in Barnsley. From there he went to Birmingham University where he studied working with computers amongst other things. While he was waiting for a job to materialise he worked nights at a dress manufacturers in Barnsley.

His job was to set up the computers to cut out different styles of dresses. One day he had a letter from an American firm that was starting a branch of their business in England so he sent them his curriculum vitae after seeing an advertisement in the newspaper. He was invited to their office in London for an interview and, by the time he'd got back home, they'd phoned to tell him he'd got the job. He told us that during his interview he was asked if he would go to work in America if they wanted him to and he had said yes. Lo and behold he'd just worked a year for them when he was asked to go, and saying nothing ventured nothing gained, off he flew. He rented a house with three other young men on the east coast of America where the sea came right up to the front door. The town was called Morris Cove. From then on he never looked back, enjoying the work and the lifestyle, going everywhere and doing everything which, when we visited, seemed to be the American way.

33. Holiday

Back at work years before I had been approached by the Secretary of C.O.S.A., which was the white collared branch of *The National Union of Mineworkers,* asking me if I would serve on the Committee. Remembering my Dad's role in the Union and how it altered our family's life I was tempted to refuse, thinking I didn't want to get into that position. So I said that I would serve on the Committee but didn't have the time to move any further up than that as at that time I had a young family and my wife had started working in a hospital in Sheffield. Pat had decided when the our family was old enough to fend for itself a little that she would like to help other people who required it. She got a job at the Middlewood Mental Hospital, to which she travelled to by bus and then train. My responsibilities within the Committee were to attend a fortnightly meeting at *The Market Hotel* in Elsecar, which wasn't far from the Workshops. I only ever drank shandies whilst I was there however.

It was about this time that I, along with many other householders, was given the opportunity of buying the Coal Board house that we were living in. After looking at all the pros and cons I decided to do so. I can remember going to the solicitor's firm in Barnsley with Pat and signing a document which said that we would be prepared to pay the Coal Board a certain sum of money out of my wage each week. I think we must have borrowed the amount of money we had to put down in the first place. Looking back I thought we must have been very brave. But, then again when I think back, we were given the money to buy our first house when we left Rose Grove to live on Caxton Street by my mother-in-law, and then we'd sold it when we came back to Elsecar. So that's where we must have got our money to buy the house.

The Coal Board house which we lived in was made of a concrete slab construction and it wasn't long before a firm came around, asking if we, the people who had bought the houses, would like to have them bricked on the outside. Then we had to borrow money from the Coal Board to have it done and pay them back each week out of my wage. You would have thought that the contractors who were doing the job would have moved us out of the house, but that would have been too easy. We had to stay in the house while it had all the concrete slabs on the outside chiselled off, living very awkwardly. We had to dodge pipe jacks which sprouted, it seemed to us, from every conceivable place. These of course had to be in position all over the house. Otherwise there wouldn't have been anything to hold the ceilings and roof in place.

My wife of course took the children and herself away to her sister's while this pandemonium was occurring and left the rest of the world to me. But everything comes to those who wait they say and it did, with new windows fitted and a veranda in place sheltering the front door. The next year when the fortnight holiday came round we decided to stay at home. Mainly because we weren't in a position to afford one, and it turned out to be a good job that we couldn't for the Coal Board. I think it had got to Tuesday in the first week of our holiday when Bill Baker came knocking on our door asking if I'd got anything planned for the next few days. I looked at him worryingly and had reason to when he asked me if I'd come into work for a few days.

"I'm on holiday Bill, as well you know!" I told him. "I'm sorry," he replied, "But there's been an accident at New Stubbin and our Manager would like you to come out and help to repair the damage." It appeared that the hydraulic rams that pushed the empty tubs into the Cage, pushing the full tubs out when the Cage landed at the surface, had decided to have a mind of their own. For some reason they had started pushing the empty tubs when the Cage was twenty feet below its landing position. This resulted in the wooden gates, which prevented people falling down the shaft when the Cages were in the shaft, being smashed to matchwood.

Normally the gates were lifted up out of the way ordinarily by the Cage when it landed at the coal landing position. Then the Banksman operated the rams after he had let the fallers take the weight of the Cage. He must have been totally mystified when he saw two empty tubs plough through the gates and hit the upcoming Cage, especially when he knew that the compressed air which operated the rams couldn't be on.

After thanking God he'd been at the other side of the shaft when the rams decided to take leave of their senses, he'd signalled the Winder to stop. Luckily the Winder had been crawling the Cage into its landing position using his reversing lever as a brake and had it nearly stopped. That, together with the short distance that the tubs had to fall, minimised the impact.

However when the damage had been checked it was found that the Cage would need considerable repairs before it would bring tubs of coal out of the pit again. The upshot was that the Cage was lifted gingerly to its landing and the full tubs of coal were pulled out. One man who witnessed the operation said it was like getting sardines out of a half opened can. The work was carried out by the usual workforce at the Colliery, wondering all the time I suspect, how on earth such a thing could have happened.

Then, as it was always an unwritten law that a spare Cage should always be ready for use in an accident such as this, it was just a matter of taking the damaged Cage off and replacing it with the spare one. Unfortunately though when they looked around for it, Houdini seemed to have visited South Yorkshire and spirited it away! After a good deal of wondering and scratching of heads someone remembered where it was; working quite happily at a nearby Colliery, probably where the gremlins had struck yet again perhaps. We assumed that they must have been so relieved to get back into production so quickly that they forgot to replace it.

After frantic phone calls to Collieries near and far proved to be of no avail, the powers-that-be were faced with the fact that it would have to be a do-it-yourself job. Of course they worked out that they themselves hadn't the space or the facilities to effect the repairs, and who had? The reason that Bill Baker came knocking at our door told us that they weren't long finding somebody who had, but it wasn't all beer and skittles to get the Cage lowered back down to the bottom of the shaft. The balance rope had to be uncoupled from underneath the Cage. This was only after it had been made able to move down to the bottom of the shaft again, as it had been knocked out of shape somewhat. Then it was fastened securely, there so that the Cage could be attached to it again once it had been repaired. Of course there was just then the matter of lifting the Cage. Girders were run inside it at the 'Low Landing' with a mobile crane and it was deposited onto a low loader.

Our work then began when it was dropped off at Elsecar Workshops. The trouble was that a lot of our workers were on holiday, and rightly so because it was our holiday weeks. In the end we had to borrow some New Stubbin workmen to help us straighten the Cage back to its former shape. The main problem was that part of the Cage had to be stripped down as that was the only way we could straighten it. The construction of course had been rivets and I remember burning the heads off the ones we wanted out and, with the help of a Striker, knocking them out. It was just a matter of straightening everything and then riveting it up to where it had been before someone (or something) had decided to turn the compressed air on before it was required. It all took time but, at long last, the Cage was back on the low loader one morning. As a treat we all went back with it to hang it in its shaft once more. Then we were given breakfast at the canteen at Parkgate Colliery. "Aren't they good to us?" we laughed.

When I finally arrived back at Elsecar Workshops the Works Manager took me home in his car. I considered it to be appreciation for a job done well, but my wife didn't thank him for keeping me from home so long. She asked him if there wasn't a law against keeping men at work for long periods as this and didn't seem to be put off with his argument that a coal mine without a cage hadn't been producing coal for quite a long time. But time and tide heals all things and soon it was only a passing memory.

34. Strike

Life became humdrum really after getting that out of the way at work, apart from not having time to spit as I had so many jobs to do. It certainly made the time flash by and before we knew where we were, after rumours that Collieries were going to close and Union leaders saying, "Shut them at your peril!" we found ourselves on strike.

I shall always remember being phoned up by another Foreman to tell me that we were on strike. All the workmen had been called out two weeks before, but all Foremen were allowed to stay on by the Union. They thought everyone would come out on strike and that the Government would have to allow Cortonwood to keep open, so all Foremen would be in place to get the men working as normal when they came back. The Coal Board had decreed that they were going to close Cortonwood Colliery so the National Union of Mineworkers had called a *General Strike*, but in a different way from all other strikes I had ever known. This one had the rules for calling a strike changed.

In all my years as a Trade Unionist, every member was given the opportunity to vote for or against a strike by a secret ballot. This had to be a majority vote for or against before a strike could be called. To my knowledge the ruling Union Officials at that time had decided that we were going to strike come hell or high water. No ballot and no explanation why; years of Union ruling blown away in the wind. Some people said that the Conservative Government, who were in power at the time, would start with Cortonwood and gradually decimate the rest of the Collieries in turn. My view was why should we change years of Union protocol that our fathers had fought for? Could it be that someone in Union authority had an idea that the vote might be against a strike?

There was another thought that I couldn't get out of my mind too. On my walk to work with my Dad he used to tell me about going on strike and how you had to be prepared to win and lose some. One thing he used to say over and over again was, "United we stand. Divided we fall". But, he also said that every Union member was entitled to cast his vote whichever way he wanted, it was his given right.

Before the strike had even been thought about a list had been drawn up by negotiations between the Colliery management and Union Officials about Foremen who would be given early retirement, what date they would retire and how much they would get when they retired. I was fortunate enough I thought to be on that list, but it was put into operation just before the strike started. The trouble was my name was taken off the list and another older Foreman, who didn't cover as many jobs as I did, fitted in. The reason I was given was that after the strike was sorted out strong Foremen would be needed to get things working back to normal. I appealed to everyone, Union and management alike, but to no avail. In the end I just gave it up as a bad job and followed my leader, even though inside my heart wasn't in it.

I went with other C.O.S.A. members, picketing Colliery Offices, appealing to clerical staff who were working to join us, as their jobs were on the line just as ours were. A fair amount of striking miners informed their local Unemployment Offices that they were on strike and would like to be given benefit as they had no money coming in. They soon got a reply by return of post saying that their Union should be giving them strike pay, but of course the Yorkshire Miners' Union never had given it and wouldn't be doing now. What they did do was to give out food vouchers.

I never accepted any though as my wife was working and we could just about manage. I still had to go down to Elsecar Mains old stocking ground coal, picking with a wheelbarrow though. I would bring it back full of coal dust, liberally laced with small stones that spat out venomously with an accompanying crack when hot. They burnt the design from our kitchen rug and blistered your legs if you didn't get out of the way quick enough. The strike was soon in trouble though. Our brother miners in Nottinghamshire decided not to join us and, despite our Union bosses entreaties to the A.E.U., they never came to our aid. We were on a hiding to nothing whichever way we looked.

We did hear at the beginning of the strike that one of the main officials of our Union had got three months supply of coke in for his central heating system, just another thing that was wrong about this strike to my mind. Inevitably after a year of hardship and belt tightening, the miners realised that they had to go back to work. They went back with Colliery brass bands playing, but had accomplished nothing apart from getting into debt and having nothing to show for a year's trouble and strife.

35. A Walk Down Memory Lane

The Coal Board, under the Government's direction of course, closed pits down, and just as quickly knocked them down. The first one was Cortonwood, as they had said would happen. I thought to myself as one of my walks took me to see it in its half torn-down state, "How long will it be before the cycle turns the full circle and we'll be wanting coal again?" Memories came flooding back when I passed a heap of dismantled debris, which lay against the end of the Fitting Shop; a length of winding rope complete with its Capel, which had been the last one to be capped here. Beside it was the circular dial complete with its arrow headed finger still coupled up to the gearing. It had been used to run off the Parkgate winding drum shaft. The finger was still pointing to the mark on the dial where the Winder had stopped the engine for the last time - the coal landing.

Then I walked to the remains of the Parkgate Pit shaft. All of its area was now filled up with concrete and I saw for the first time in daylight the huge air vents which surrounded its diameter. This shaft was deepest one at the Colliery. I had only had a view of these vents when we went into its low landing, which had had a big double door with a slide in it to allow you to balance the air pressure.

At the shaft side we kept two big girders. Each would be balanced in their centre on a four wheeled tram, which we ran inside the Cage when we wanted to change the suspension gear. Once we had run them in the Winder gradually lowered the Cage on to them, whereby all the gear dropped on the roof of it. Then we signalled him to stop when we had enough slack to clamp and tie the winding rope off. Finally we were able to uncouple the capel from all the gear. We would strip off all the old and would replaced it with the new gear, which had been checked and certified as being safe to use. All this was done working in the light of our cap lamps, which was why I never got a good view of the vents.

All the Workshops were still standing at that time when I walked round what was left of the Colliery. The dismantlers had started to wreck the headgear and the shafts first. I went into the Blacksmiths' Shop first and found that hardly anything had changed since I had left to go to Elsecar Workshops. There were the same hearths and machinery, all now destined to end up in some scrap yard. Even the big wooden tool boxes remained at the side of each furnace, and I remembered the first time that I'd sat on one, kicking my heels and wondering what was in store for me.

When I looked inside one it was still full of tools, as though the Blacksmith would be coming to use them on the next shift. Alas no more. The steel door that led into the Fitting Shop was open and when I went through a different sight awaited me. All the machines that used to stand in line at the side of the Shop, like a row of shining teeth, now looked as though a mad dentist had been allowed to run amok amongst them, pulling different ones out. Very few were left, either moved to another Colliery or delivered to a nearby scrap heap, leaving blank spaces never to be filled again. That was the last time I saw Cortonwood Colliery whole. The next time it looked like an old battlefield and I couldn't for the life of me remember where different things had been.

Back at Elsecar Workshops we went about our work with the knowledge that, if Collieries closed, it wouldn't be long before our time would come. I got the message quicker than anybody else. As soon as I got back to work the Cost Office wanted information about different products that we'd been making for Collieries, the time it took to make them, materials that were required and drawings of them. All these things had to be in their hands quickly, but it would take them time to get them together and, to my mind, we didn't have time on their side. The reason for this was the Powers That Be had been contacting outside manufacturers to make these things and that meant that, as a Workshop, we were on our way out.

It wasn't long before all the workforce were invited to a meeting in the Machine Shop chaired by the Work's Superintendent to tell us that was going to happen. I can recall the scene now, people standing against the walls and somewhere they could, sitting down. He began by telling us how sorry he was but that the time had come for us to close down. To that end people who were near retirement age would be finishing early and others who weren't would be transferred to other Workshops, with the Coal Board taking care of their transport to work.

When Foremen finished work staff were invited to witness a presentation by the management after a 'whip round', which the collection was called. Usually the Foremen's wives were sent a bouquet, usually delivered by a female member of staff. I remember the last one I went to was Bill Baker's when he retired from the Planning Office. He was presented with a collapsible workbench and we were all photographed in a group around him and it. Alas, when it came to my turn, so many Foremen were retiring at that one time that I was simply presented with a letter by the internal mailman, telling me that my services to the Coal Board over the years had been truly appreciated. What made it a mockery in my eyes was that these letters had been run off on a copying machine and names written in, not much appreciation there to my mind was there!

Everybody who was going to retire had been interviewed about their pension and told what they would be entitled to if they opted to be paid by a lump sum, or how much they would get if they wanted to get paid weekly. We were given a period of time to think about it and then had to let them know when we'd made our minds up which way we wanted to be paid. Then we were told the date when we would finish.

I shall always remember the day I finished work. After dinner a van driver came into my Office who said that he'd been sent from Manvers Pool. This was the Depot where all the transport was requested by our Area. I knew this young man very well as he'd done a lot of work for us, but I was mystified why he'd come and told him so. He replied, "I've been requested by your Manager to come to see you and wish you a happy retirement. I'm also to take whatever you want home from this Shop in my van." It didn't take very long for me to make my mind up. I remembered the last time, taking something home from the Coal Board, and my visit to the 'Sheffield Assizes' with all the heartache it had caused. And so I decided there was nothing that I wanted. I gathered everything that belonged to me out of my desk and told him all I required was a lift home.

My last visit to the place where I started my working life at the Cortonwood Colliery was to find it had been transformed into a shopping centre, which was ringed by grass-seeded spoil heaps, all of them made over the years by the material that couldn't be used. But I was pleased to see in one store, a large photograph of the Vesting Day Ceremony at Cortonwood, which was taken at the side of the Lamp

Room. It portrayed all the Union Officials, including my Dad in the centre. Beside him stood the oldest workman and the youngest, holding the board on which proclaimed the changeover from the Masters to the Men.

www.ingramcontent.com/pod-product-compliance
Ingram Content Group UK Ltd.
Pitfield, Milton Keynes, MK11 3LW, UK
UKHW020241250726
13967UKWH00001B/485